An Outline of Sociology as Applied to Medicine

An Outline of Sociology as Applied to Medicine

Third edition

David Armstrong   MB MSc PhD FFCM

Reader in Sociology as Applied to Medicine,
United Medical and Dental Schools of Guy's
and St. Thomas' Hospitals, London University

WRIGHT
London   Boston   Singapore   Sydney   Toronto   Wellington

Wright
is an imprint of Butterworth–Heinemann Ltd

 PART OF REED INTERNATIONAL P.L.C.

First edition published by John Wright 1980
Second edition 1983
Third edition 1989
Reprinted 1990

British Library Cataloguing in Publication Data

Armstrong, David, *1947–*
    An outline of sociology as applied to medicine – 3rd ed
    1. Man. Health. Social aspects
    I. Title
    362.1′042

ISBN 0-7236-1691-4

Library of Congress Cataloging in Publication Data

Armstrong, David, 1947 – June 3 –
    An outline of sociology as applied to medicine.

    Bibliography: P. 131
    Includes index.
    1. Social medicine,   I. Title.
RA418.A725   1989   362.1′042   89-882
ISBN 0-7236-1691-4

Composition by Genesis Typesetting, Laser Quay, Rochester, Kent
Printed in Great Britain at the University Press, Cambridge

Preface to the third edition

Since the last edition, published in 1983, there have been changes in medical sociology as well as in medicine and in medical education. In the light of these I have substantially rewritten and rearranged most of the chapters, hopefully to provide a more coherent and relevant overview of the subject.

As in the past, the emphasis is on providing a framework for understanding the relationship between health care and the society in which it occurs. This relationship takes various forms and knowledge of them should help in understanding the origins, nature and context of illness in society, as well as in the care of individual patients.

I am grateful to the students who have influenced the course and form of this book and also to my colleagues Nicky Britten, on the sociological side, and John Weinman, on the psychological, who have freely given help and advice at various points. I must record a special thanks to Myfanwy Morgan with whom I have closely collaborated in the teaching at UMDS: I owe her many of the (better) ideas in the book. I would also like to thank Carol Butterfield who carefully typed the manuscript; and, as always, my wife, Pauline, for her support, tolerance and encouragement.

David Armstrong
April 1989

Contents

1

Introduction

Until about 200 years ago humoral theories of illness dominated clinical practice, but these were swept away at the turn of the eighteenth century by a new type of medicine which maintained that illness existed in the form of a discrete pathological lesion inside the body (Foucault, 1963). In keeping with this new framework for looking at illness, the practice of medicine changed quite radically: the clinical examination was introduced to search for disease, post-mortems became common to identify precisely the disease that had caused death, and the hospital emerged as a place for patients to receive treatment.

This new model of disease – often called the biomedical because it reduces illness to a biological abnormality inside the body – has led to enormous resources being invested in the careful examination of anatomical and physiological processes, both normal and abnormal, to identify the pathological basis of many diseases; in addition the pharmacological revolution, especially since the Second World War, has given doctors a wide range of weapons with which to fight disease. Yet some illnesses have failed to succumb to this biomedical analysis. For example, for nearly 200 years the brain tissues of the mentally disturbed have been closely scrutinized after death to find the organic roots of their illness, but without success.

Biomedicine continues to hold out hope that eventually psychiatric disorder will be explained in terms of cerebral pathological lesions; others have argued that the search for a full organic explanation of psychiatric morbidity is futile. No matter how closely the internal electronics of a television set are examined they will never reveal an adequate understanding of the type and variety of programmes being shown; in the same way, an examination of the brain, no matter how detailed, can never succeed in explaining why someone has a certain thought, or holds a religious or political belief, or speaks a particular language. In other words there seem to be aspects of human functioning which fall outside the classical biomedical model. Certainly there may be neurophysiological correlates of ideas, thoughts, culture, moods, etc., but these biological correlates cannot explain the origins of the content of these mental processes.

Historically the biomedical model of illness has been extremely successful. Yet in some ways it has been too successful in that it has crowded out alternative explanations and understandings of the nature of illness. The arguments in the rest of this book, which attempt to identify some deficiencies of the biomedical model and to describe various ways that the social world relates to illness, is an attempt to help redress the balance.

● References

Foucault, M. (1963) *The Birth of the Clinic: An Archeology of Medical Perception,* Tavistock, London

2

Going to the doctor

The traditional medical model holds that disease is a lesion inside the human body which produces two types of indicator of its presence:

1. *Symptoms*: those feeling states patients experience which alert them to the possibility that all is not well.
2. *Signs*: those pointers the doctor identifies which signify the existence of the underlying pathological lesion.

The doctor is therefore a sort of detective who infers the existence of the disease from the outward clues of its presence. In this model the patient is required to play a very specific role, namely bring and report the symptom to the doctor so that the detective work can proceed. Unfortunately for the efficient working of this model, people do not behave according to expectations in that they do not seem to use symptoms as triggers to seek help. This can be seen in two illustrations:

1. There are people who fail to go the doctor, or go very late despite experiencing symptoms of serious disease. This group constitutes what has been termed the 'clinical iceberg', in that it seems that there are more people who have serious symptomatic disease not under medical care than there are receiving treatment (Last, 1963).
2. There are people who attend the doctor with trivial or relatively minor complaints. Some general practitioners have reported that between a third and a half of their patients fall into this category (Cartwright and Anderson, 1981).

What then is the relationship between symptoms and the decision to consult a doctor?

● **The experience of symptoms**

A novel survey, published in 1954, described the views on health of some 500 families in a small American town (Koos, 1954). The study reported that people seemed to experience symptoms much more frequently than their rate of medical consultations would indicate. The researchers were surprised at this finding because they had assumed, as had medicine for a century and a half, that symptoms as indicators of disease almost invariably led to help-seeking behaviour.

In the following years other researchers found similar results. Sometimes patients were shown a checklist of symptoms and asked whether they had experienced any of these: for example, one such survey found that adults could recall on average about four symptoms in the previous two weeks (Dunnell and Cartwright, 1972). Other surveys simply asked whether any symptoms had been experienced in a certain time period, making the assumption that as it was patients who made the decision whether or not to view a symptom as serious, they were best able to judge what was to count as a symptom in the first place. And finally some researchers persuaded people to keep a daily 'health diary' of the symptoms they experienced and many found that noting down at least one symptom every day was not uncommon (Banks *et al.*, 1975).

Table 2.1 Ratio of symptom episodes to consultations. (After Banks *et al.*, 1975)

Headache	184:1
Backache	52:1
Emotional problem	46:1
Abdominal pain	28:1
Sore throat	18:1
Pain in chest	14:1

Table 2.1 shows the results of one study of patients' reported symptoms and their decision to consult a doctor. It can be seen that the decision to seek medical advice was a relatively rare occurrence even for supposedly serious symptoms such as chest pain.

In summary, very few of the symptoms which people reported in these studies of symptom prevalence were actually taken to the doctor; whereas people seem to report experiencing several symptoms a week, they only go to see the doctor on average about three or four times a year. Thus it would seem that patients must subject their symptoms to some form of evaluation or interpretation before deciding to seek medical advice.

● **Illness behaviour**

In 1960 the notion of 'illness behaviour' was advanced to explain the process by which patients reached the doctor (Mechanic and Volkart, 1960). Illness behaviour was a term given to 'the ways in which given symptoms may be differentially perceived, evaluated and acted upon (or not acted upon) by different kinds of person' (Mechanic, 1962).

Medicine, Mechanic observed, had the task of 'effecting the arrival of "ill" persons at medical settings so that treatment can be effectively administered'. The means of achieving this was by eliminating the factors preventing attendance through patient education: 'one of the prime functions of public health programmes is to teach populations to accept and behave in accordance with the definitions made by the medical profession'.

But first, the factors affecting the 'career' of moving from being a well person to being an ill patient had to be better understood. The 'symptom' iceberg had shown that as symptoms were so widely distributed they could not be the precise trigger which took people to the doctor; nor did it seem to be the symptom's severity or seriousness, as the 'clinical' iceberg contained patients with serious disease, and accompanying symptoms, who chose not to go to the doctor.

Following on Mechanic's original work, various studies have explored the factors which encourage or hinder people's attendance at medical facilities. The process of becoming a patient was seen to have various stages. Clearly not every stage may be important in bringing the patient to the doctor, but it can be useful to consider the process as a series of potential questions posed by every patient.

Are my symptoms normal or abnormal?

Symptoms and their perceived danger are subjected to some form of evaluation. Because frequent background symptoms are a normal event for most people, it tends to be the symptom which is unusual or atypical in form or context which is seen as most threatening.

1. Certain symptoms are classified as normal probably because of their wide prevalence in society. Headaches for example are so common that only about 1 in 200 is presented to the doctor; those that turn up are presumably unusual in some way, perhaps in terms of 'normal' frequency or context.
2. Normality may not only be defined by reference to the total society but also to smaller groupings within the community. Every member of a society belongs to a number of such sub-groups and will therefore tend to accept the expectations of these groups with regard to symptoms and illness. For example, one of the expectations of old age is that more general aches and pains will be experienced than in younger people. The experience of such symptoms may be seen as normal by many old people and many may be tolerated without bothering the doctor.

   Even when the patient presents to the doctor, this 'normalization' may block the emergence of important diagnostic information. While taking a medical history from a patient who smokes it is not uncommon to find that he denies having a cough. On prompting he (and, increasingly, she) often remonstrates, 'Oh, its only a smoker's cough'. The patient has interpreted 'Do you have a cough?' as 'Do you have an abnormal cough?' to which, for a patient who coughs every morning and perhaps lives in a household of similar people, the answer is no.
3. Earlier events may also be called upon to normalize the presence of a symptom. For example, a rodent ulcer might be seen as a bruise which has not healed from an earlier bump on the forehead or the lump of a breast cancer might be explained away by some half-forgotten injury; as it grows very slowly in size its characteristics are not seen as abnormal as it increasingly 'has always been like that'. It is sometimes only when the cancer breaks down and fungates that the patient comes to the doctor complaining of the abnormal and socially unacceptable smell.

Should I go to the doctor on this occasion?

The significance of symptoms to the patient seems to lie in whether they are perceived as 'normal' or 'abnormal'. It seems therefore it is not the symptoms themselves which take people to the doctor but the assessment of them. It is possible to break this assessment down into what Zola suggests are five 'social triggers' which together encompass the various ways in which symptoms come to be seen as abnormal (Zola, 1973). They are:

1. *Perceived interference with vocational or physical activity.* As vocational or physical activity is a part of 'normal' life then symptoms which interfere with it must be abnormal. Allowances must be made however for the type of work or activity: a cut finger may interfere more with a typist than a car driver and some physical disability may only become apparent to a sedentary office worker if he plays a game of football one day.
2. *Perceived interference with social or personal relations.* Similarly, symptoms which interfere with normal social interaction will be more likely to cause concern. Consideration must be given to the patient's usual pattern of interaction which may differ for different occupations, ages, life styles, etc.
3. *The occurrence of an interpersonal crisis.* An interpersonal crisis can upset the everyday equilibrium people seem to have with many of their symptoms. Some change in personal relationships can change the perception of an otherwise minor symptom or seemingly decrease the tolerance to chronic pain or disability. The patient with long-standing osteoarthritis who presents with joint pain after 'coping' for a long period may in fact be triggered by a domestic crisis rather than by an exacerbation of the underlying condition.
4. *A kind of temporalizing of symptomatology.* Although the symptom may or may not interfere with work or social relations it may still be seen as unusual or ambiguous. Some deadline may then be set for the symptom. This may be a time deadline such as, 'If this symptom has not disappeared by Monday then I shall go to the doctor', or it may be a frequency deadline such as, 'If I have more than two nose bleeds this week . . . .'.
5. *Sanctioning.* Sanctioning refers to pressure from friends or relatives to visit the doctor. It is not uncommon for a patient to open the consultation with, 'I did not want to bother you but . . . insisted I should come'.

What else can I do?

There are a variety of alternative strategies – which are not necessarily mutually exclusive – available for people who experience symptoms. These are covered in more detail in Chapter 10.

1. Ignore the symptoms.
2. The patient may consult with friends and relatives. It has been suggested that advice given by friends and relatives constitutes a *lay referral system,* analogous to the medical system, in which the patient is referred to lay consultants with successively greater claim to knowledge or experience of the symptom in question. It has also been suggested that the lay referral system for a tight-knit community may act as an alternative health care system. As most symptoms are probably self-limiting this alternative system may, in effect, limit the demand for medical services.
3. The patient may use self-medication or self-help.
4. The patient may consult with professional health care practitioners, most commonly with their general practitioner.

Whether course (4) is pursued and the official medical services consulted can be seen as a process by which the patient compares the relative costs and benefits of such action.

What are the costs and benefits of seeing the doctor?

The first decision concerns the perceived value of going to the doctor: will he or she be able to do anything for the problem? Besides offering sympathy and reassurance the doctor has two, more formal, functions through which the patient can be helped.

1. The first is therapeutic: the doctor can offer some form of treatment which may benefit the patient. Patients may have their own idea of what treatment the doctor can offer and this may influence the decision to consult. Some people consult their doctor expecting cures and treatments which do not exist; alternatively many people do not consult because they feel the doctor cannot do anything for them. One study reported that among a group of patients in the year before their death many symptoms were experienced for which no medical advice was sought; 29% of these symptoms were described as 'very distressing' and 37% had been present for a year or more (Cartwright *et al.*, 1973).

2. The second way in which the doctor can help the patient is to ease the transition from being a 'person' to being a 'patient'. Although people may feel unwell they may not be socially accepted as being ill, for example by their employers, unless a doctor 'legitimates' the illness. In Western society only the doctor has the social authority to legitimate illness and admit the person to what Parsons described as the 'sick role' (see also Chapter 15). According to Parsons, in accepting the sick role the patient gains two benefits but is expected to fulfil two obligations (Parsons, 1951). These are:

   (a) The patient is temporarily excused his or her normal role. Gaining a sickness absence certificate from the doctor is the obvious way in which the expectation is met. Merely visiting the doctor however confers some legitimacy on a claim to be sick. Whereas 'feeling unwell' might be treated sceptically by friends and colleagues, a visit to the doctor may be sufficient to gain credibility.

   (b) The patient is not responsible for his or her illness. Not being held responsible for the illness relieves the patient of a considerable burden in our society. In some other societies the patient may be held responsible in that, for example, the illness might be believed to be a punishment for some past crime or transgression.

   (c) The patient must want to get well. By gaining two advantages from the sick role the patient must undertake two obligations. The first is his recognition that the sick role is a temporary status which he must want to leave behind. If he apparently does not want to get well then instead of the sick role being conferred by the doctor a label of 'malingering' may be used.

   (d) The patient must cooperate with technically competent help. The fact that it is only the doctor who can legitimately confer the sick role in our society ensures that 'technically competent help' tends to be confined to the official medical services. A patient who chooses to defer to a lay person with claims to medical knowledge, in preference to a medical practitioner, is judged as not fulfilling one of the basic obligations of the sick role.

While undoubtedly the notion of the sick role is very useful in understanding the behaviour of many people who consult their doctor, its use is circumscribed by those patients who for various reasons are unable to fulfil all the expectations and obligations which it entails. This has been noted as particularly pertinent for those with a chronic illness who are both unable and unlikely to meet several of the obligations – although this failure to encompass patients with chronic illness may explain why doctors tend to be better disposed to those 'acute' specialties, such as general medicine and surgery, compared with those dealing with chronic problems such as geriatrics.

The sick role confers both obligations and expectations on the patient. Expectations, such as being excused normal work, may be of benefit to the patient whereas certain of the obligations such as having to cooperate with the doctor may be counted as a social cost. This cost is only one of many to be found in actually using a health service. Other costs are found even when there is no financial charge at the point of use and these, whether they are waiting lists, inconvenient surgery hours or the time needed to go to the doctor, tend to act as disincentives to use the service.

The other potential cost of using the health service is the approachability of the doctor. Undoubtedly many patients are put off going to doctors because they believe they will not be sympathetic to their particular complaint. It has been found, for example, that many patients withhold serious complaints from the doctor because of apparent busyness or disinterest. It has also been suggested that the wide variation in the numbers of patients presenting with a sexual problem to different doctors is itself a product of the doctor's approachability. Patients quickly establish whether their doctor will handle a sexual problem with sympathy and understanding or whether he or she will dismiss it or be embarrassed by it, and these perceptions may well affect their decision to seek help.

● **Importance of illness behaviour for the doctor**

The answer to the question, 'Why do people go to the doctor?' is not a simple one. Studies in the field of illness behaviour have shown that seeking medical help is not necessarily related to the occurrence or severity of a symptom. The way in which a symptom is 'processed', both in individual and social terms, will determine what action is finally taken. Here this action has been described as a 'decision-making process' on the part of the patient. Of course not all patients follow this pattern or take all these factors into consideration. Their decision may not even seem rational to doctors, but then they may not be aware of the often complex reasoning which brings a patient to the consultation. The patient who seems off-hand, the patient who says he or she did not want to come but was sent, the patient who hands over a piece of notepaper with a list of symptoms, are all to be understood in the context of a decision-making process which has often gone on several days before the patient actually reaches the doctor. To establish during the interview why the patient has come at the particular time may be of great value in both understanding and managing the presenting problem.

Perhaps the patient has unrealistic expectations of the doctor's ability and shows unusual tolerance of different symptoms. The social trigger may give some clue as to the other reasons why a patient has consulted besides the presenting complaint. A patient may have failed to keep an appointment because the surgery was too far away, because the receptionist was too brusque or because the doctor did not offer the expected sympathy last time.

While the doctor always enquires of the particular presenting problem so as to infer the nature of the underlying pathological lesion, there is, also, always a 'second diagnosis' to be made: 'Why did the patient come *now*?'. Patients very rarely come to the doctor immediately a symptom starts; most delay and wait hours, days or weeks, even months or years. For example, patients with the chest pain of a heart attack delay an average of ten hours before seeking medical advice, and even those with a past history of ischaemic heart disease, who should be more aware of the significance of chest pain, act no quicker (Rawles and Haites, 1988); no doubt many never seek help at all. In many cases the actual process of becoming ill that has been described above may be more important in understanding and managing the patient's problems than the illness itself.

- ### Illness behaviour and the medical model
During the 1970s three important challenges emerged to the traditional illness behaviour model which had tried to describe the various ways that patients respond to symptoms. These challenges came from:

1. Psychophysiological studies.
2. Interpretive studies.
3. Anthropological studies.

Psychophysiological studies

Traditionally, medicine linked symptoms to underlying pathophysiological processes, and ultimately to diseases. Tiredness suggested reduced oxygen carrying capacity of the circulatory system – perhaps anaemia – or low thyroxine, or chronic infection. Pain might arise from inflammation, or from ischaemia. In other words a symptom was the outward manifestation of an underlying pathology. And yet this apparent connection between symptom and skin-encapsulated biological processes has, in recent years, not seemed so fixed.

First, it has become clear that patients can experience a wide variety of symptoms without any apparent underlying lesion: in many instances of angina the coronary arteries seem normal; in half the cases of appendicitis the appendix is not inflamed; in most cases of backache no structural lesion can be found; tiredness seems more associated with low affect than with anaemia; and so on. Of course it can be argued that in many of these cases it is just a matter of time before the true underlying lesion is identified, but nevertheless the range and extent of these anomalies is very wide, and certainly at the moment many cannot be explained by the logic of the traditional biomedical model.

Second, there have been laboratory studies of the effect of physiological change on symptom perception which suggest there is a rather poor correlation between the two. People seem to be very poor discriminators of their underlying physiological state (Pennebaker, 1984).

Third, psychological evidence on the experience of pain suggests that the connection between tissue damage and pain is not necessarily linear. Thus in his classic study of pain in wounded soldiers, Beecher found that the circumstances surrounding the pain – for example, whether they would be returning home or not – was an important factor in the amount of pain that was experienced (Beecher, 1959). Similarly Egbert showed that postoperative pain could be reduced simply by explaining the surgical procedures to the patient before the operation (Egbert *et al.*, 1964).

These various studies of pain conform to the 'gate control theory' which claims that the experience of pain might or might not be triggered by peripheral nerve endings, but that the actual pain is mediated by 'central' brain processing (Melzack and Wall, 1965). In other words, the psychological and social state of the individual has a major influence on the pain experienced.

Taken together these various studies and observations – clinical, physiological and psychological – suggest that symptoms should not be regarded as sort of 'pop-up' indicators of physical abnormality. Indeed symptoms are percepts; they are interpretations by the mind of what is going on in the body. Certainly some of these percepts are closely linked to bodily malfunction – no doubt there is evolutionary logic to that – but equally many percepts would seem to have little direct relationship to what is going on inside the body.

This view of symptoms challenges many traditional medical assumptions, but also some of the arguments of the classical illness behaviour model. Symptoms are not simply present or not present; they may even become present if the person is asked to think about them. Moreover people cannot be said to 'interpret symptoms' because symptoms are already interpretations (otherwise it is a case of interpreting interpretations!). Believing oneself to be ill or in need of medical advice is therefore a more complex process than the simple model of illness behaviour might suggest.

Interpretive studies   *symptoms are interpretations*

The assumption of illness behaviour, like medicine before it, was that symptoms were 'given': patients had symptoms or they did not. Thus it was possible to use questionnaires, checklists and diaries to record the existence of symptoms and calculate their number and type. But is the presence of a symptom that simple?

During the 1970s new approaches to investigating people's experiences were developed which attempted to get at the respondent's own meanings. In many ways the traditional closed question survey either incorporated the researcher's meanings or pushed the respondent's own views into an inappropriate box. Thus people could be persuaded to provide an answer to the question: 'How many symptoms have you experienced last week?', but how valid was the response if they could not explain the details and nuances of that experience?

The new approaches to exploring the experience of illness relied on in-depth interviews to establish the psychosocial context that surrounded the emergence of symptoms into consciousness. These studies found a complex exploration and negotiation of experience and meanings, which the acceptance of symptoms as 'given' had failed to illuminate (Locker, 1981). Patients seemed to be using their own idiosyncratic personal constructs to evaluate and interpret bodily feelings.

Anthropological studies

When medical anthropologists investigated the explanatory models of illness used in non-industrialized societies they found that people seem to need answers to such questions as 'Why me?', 'What caused the illness?', 'Why did it begin at this particular time?', 'What will be the outcome of this illness?' and 'What should be done about it?'. It was then realized that these sorts of questions were asked by *all* patients including those in Western industrialized societies. The answers which different patients provide for these questions are known as lay theories of illness or patient's explanatory models.

The origin of individual lay theories is probably threefold:

1. *Idiosyncratic,* based on the patient's own observations and experiences.
2. *Popular,* derived from the 'lay health system'. The social network (or lay referral system, see p. 6) itself sustains various belief systems and explanatory models of illness.
3. *Expert* models of illness, in the main from biomedicine, have an influence on lay theories but obviously those aspects of expert knowledge which are integrated into a lay context may still appear incoherent to the experts themselves. Indeed experts may have their own lay theories which might be quite opposed to the theories they advance while in the role of expert.

Lay theories have been investigated in a variety of diseases. The range of these studies can be shown by citing some findings from four of them:

1. One study found that a sample of less well-educated working class mothers tended to report a fatalistic view of the aetiology of illness. These views would have particular relevance for health education programmes which are based on the notion of disease prevention (Pill and Stott, 1982).
2. Another study of beliefs about the causes of cancer found that a group of patients with cancer had stronger beliefs that cancer had little to do with personal behaviour (many thought it was inherited) than a matched group of patients without cancer. The authors suggested that this particular belief was probably a means of defending against self-blame as a mechanism of coping with a terminal illness (Linn *et al.,* 1982).
3. An investigation of what patients with high blood pressure thought the term 'hypertension' meant found that many believed it was caused by too much 'tension' or stress in their lives. Despite the lack of scientific supporting evidence it was also found that even the experts' model (of the doctors) was sympathetic to the role of stress as an aetiological agent (Blumhagen, 1980).
4. Finally, a study of lay beliefs about upper respiratory tract infection, particularly as the basis of the aphorism 'feed a cold, starve a fever', found that such illnesses were analysed in terms of hot–cold and wet–dry to establish the supposed origin of the illness, the meaning of its symptoms and the most appropriate remedies. Again the correspondences between the lay theories and the apparently more 'objective' expert models were often marked (Helman, 1978).

Lay theories are often difficult to pin down because they vary so much between people and within the same person over time. Nevertheless they are important because they affect health behaviour and doctor–patient interaction. These arguments would suggest that the patient does not come to the doctor with the odd isolated symptom but with a comprehensive belief system which in its range and power rivals the biomedical scientific belief system of the doctor. Therefore, although on the surface the doctor–patient relationship might be characterized by common interests and a common goal, it can be seen to represent a meeting of very different belief systems.

These new insights into the nature of symptoms and illness have many implications for medicine. The exact role of symptoms – even when they are taken to the doctor – in signifying disease is much less clear than the biomedical model would suppose (see Chapter 9). But in terms of the traditional illness behaviour which exhorted the doctor to make a second diagnosis of 'Why has this patient come now?', it is possible to add another question: 'What are the patient's explanatory models which brought about this visit and what implications do they have for the management of the problem?' (Kleinman *et al.*, 1978).

● References

Banks, M. H., Beresford, S. A. A., Morrell, D. C. *et al.* (1975) Factors influencing demand for primary medical care in women aged 20–44. *International Journal of Epidemiology,* **4**, 189–195

Beecher, H. R. (1959) *Measurement of Subjective Responses,* Oxford University Press, Oxford

Blumhagen, D. (1980) Hyper-tension: a folk illness with a medical name. *Culture Medicine and Psychiatry,* **4**, 197–227

Cartwright, A. and Anderson, R. (1981) *General Practice Revisited,* Tavistock, London

Cartwright, A., Hockey, L. and Anderson, J. L. (1973) *Life Before Death,* Routledge and Kegan Paul, London

Dunnell, K. and Cartwright, A. (1972) *Medicine Takers, Prescribers and Hoarders,* Routledge and Kegan Paul, London

Egbert, L. D., Battit, G. E., Welch, C. E. *et al.* (1964) Reduction of postoperative pain by encouragement and instruction of patients. *New England Journal of Medicine,* **170**, 825–827

Helman, C. (1978) 'Feed a cold starve a fever' – folk models of infection in an English suburban community and their relation to medical treatment. *Culture Medicine and Psychiatry,* **2**, 107–137

Kleinman, A., Eisenberg, L. and Good, B. (1978) Culture, illness and cure. *Annals of Internal Medicine,* **88**, 251–259

Koos, E. (1954) *The Health of Regionsville: What the People Felt and Did About It,* Columbia University Press, New York

Last, J. M. (1963) The clinical iceberg: completing the clinical picture in general practice. *Lancet,* **ii**, 28–30

Linn, M. W., Linn, B. S. and Stein, S. R. (1982) Beliefs about causes of cancer in cancer patients. *Social Science and Medicine,* **16**, 835–839

Locker, D. (1981) *Symptoms and Illness: The Cognitive Organization of Disorder,* Tavistock, London

Mechanic, D. (1962) The concept of illness behaviour. *Journal of Chronic Diseases,* **15**, 189–194

Mechanic, D. and Volkart, E. H. (1960) Illness behaviour and medical diagnosis. *Journal of Health and Human Behaviour,* **1**, 86-94

Melzack, R. and Wall, P. D. (1965) Pain mechanisms: a new theory. *Science,* **150**, 971

Parsons, T. (1951) *The Social System,* Free Press, New York

Pennebaker, J. W. (1984) Accuracy of symptom perception. In *Handbook of Psychology and Health,* vol. IV (eds A. Baum *et al.*), Erlbaum, New Jersey

Pill, R. and Stott, N. C. H. (1982) Concepts of illness causation and responsibility: some preliminary data from a sample of working class mothers. *Social Science and Medicine,* **16,** 315–322

Rawles, J. M. and Haites, N. E. (1988) Patient and general practitioner delays in acute myocardial infarcts. *British Medical Journal,* **296,** 882–884

Zola, I. K. (1973) Pathways to the doctor: from person to patient. *Social Science and Medicine,* **7,** 677–689

3

Measuring health and illness

Research in the field of illness behaviour has shown that patients make their own personal assessments of their health in the process of deciding whether to contact health services. This patient view is not necessarily the same as the medical view of health: it is possible for a patient to feel healthy and a doctor to think otherwise, and vice versa. In effect doctor and patient might be said to be assessing different components of health – one the biomedical basis, the other the more subjective impact.

This difference of perspective between doctor and patient reflects the fact that health has many dimensions. Ideally any definition or measurement of health needs to take account of these different components. In practice there is no single measure of health which embraces them all, but rather a variety of different ones each with their own strengths and weaknesses.

• Mortality

Crude death rates

With the registration of all deaths in the mid-nineteenth century, it became possible to establish the mortality experience of the whole population. At first it was simply a question of adding together all deaths to produce an overall figure, so enabling the mortality in one year or one community to be compared with the mortality in another.

The problem with these mortality figures was that the population 'at risk' of dying might vary considerably from year to year or between different communities; the mortality figure therefore needed to be expressed as a rate per number at risk. To achieve this the raw number of deaths was divided by the denominator of the population's size. This produced what is called the 'crude mortality rate'.

Age/sex corrected mortality rates

The crude mortality rate is one measure of illness in a community which allows populations of differing sizes to be compared. But while it allows for the numbers in different populations, it ignores the fact that the age and sex make-up may be very different. Many countries have areas which are popular with elderly and retired people, and these areas, as might be expected, tend to have high crude mortality rates. However, it is possible that the actual mortality, allowing for this age and sex difference, is not significantly higher than in another part of the country. This has led demographers to standardize the death rate by allowing for the age and sex mix of the underlying population.

Age and cause-specific mortality rates

The analysis of a population's mortality was taken a step further with a closer look at the age-specific death rates and the causes of death. Particularly in international comparisons, the infant mortality rate has regularly been used to compare the health status of different countries. Equally various patterns can be identified, both over time and between geographical areas, in the types of illness that kill people.

Mortality rates in general have major advantages as measures of health:

1. They are routinely available by age, sex and geographical area.
2. The overall figures tend to be very reliable given that death is an unambiguous state.

However they also have serious disadvantages:

1. The ascription of a cause to each death seems to vary with changes in knowledge and fashion. Thus, to some extent, the differences in the cause of death over time and between geographical areas may be the consequence of different reporting procedures from clinicians, pathologists and coroners.
2. They do not indicate the amount of *morbidity*, i.e. illness, in the population. It is possible for a population to have relatively low mortality rates yet large numbers of people with chronic illnesses such as osteoarthritis which do not cause death yet are seriously debilitating. In fact most illnesses do not produce death and therefore are not embraced by mortality statistics.

What is therefore needed is a measure of illness itself.

●   Morbidity prevalence studies

As biomedicine has traditionally analysed illness in terms of pathology-based diseases, then measuring diseases directly would seem to be a good way of assessing the health of a population. In principle this can be done using community prevalence surveys in which random samples of the population are assessed for their health status. In practice such surveys pose several difficulties:

1. They are very expensive: large numbers of health personnel are needed to carry them out.
2. There is a difficulty in defining what is a disease for the purposes of the study.
3. It is difficult to allow for severity – two patients may have the same disease but be differently incapacitated by it.
4. There is a problem of data comparability in that it is difficult to add and manipulate different diagnoses. For example, if one community has ten cases of ischaemic heart disease and another ten cases of chronic bronchitis, which is the healthier?

These limitations mean that large-scale community prevalence studies to measure the health of a population are uncommon, and when they do occur they tend to focus on individual diseases which have easy and specific diagnostic tests (such as diabetes).

The exception to this general rule is psychiatric disorder. The diagnosis of mental illness does not require a technical diagnostic test but relies on the patient's response to the psychiatrist's questions. This has led psychiatrists to try and reproduce the diagnostic interview in a questionnaire. There are now many such questionnaires in existence, perhaps one of the best known being the General Health Questionnaire which is used to pick up cases of anxiety and depression.

● **Sickness absence rates**

A good measure of health would reduce all illness to a simple figure which could then be standardized by using a common denominator: the health status in one population could then be compared with another. Sickness absence figures reduce illness to a number of days lost from work through illness. This figure is divided by the number of days worked to establish a rate, which can then be used to compare two or more populations or one population over time.

While sickness absence rates are regularly collected, and can be obtained for specific geographical areas or time periods, there are problems with their validity.

1. They are known to be affected by illness behaviour. Thus it seems likely that some people – and there may be a systematic pattern – are more likely to seek work absence for a illness than other people.
2. The requirements for certification change over time and vary for different occupations. Thus a person in an occupation which provides automatic sickness cover may be less likely to register as ill than someone who needs to register to obtain sick pay.
3. Perhaps most significant of all, sickness absence figures only cover that proportion of the population in the workforce. In other words it excludes children, the unemployed, the elderly and housewives who, in comparison with the rest of the population, are believed in general to be sicker. In effect, at best sickness absence rates measure the amount of sickness in the healthiest group in the population.

For these reasons sickness absence is judged a very limited measure of health.

● **Caseload**

When people are ill they may choose to go to see their doctor. Thus one method of measuring illness would be to count the number of times patients in a population visit their general practitioner or attend hospital. Such data could be obtained from hospital and general practice statistics.

Such caseload figures, however, reflect three different phenomena:

1. They obviously must reflect health need, which is the phenomenon which the health measure wishes to encompass.

2. Caseload figures also reflect illness behaviour. It is now well established that many patients with serious illness choose not to seek help from health services, while many with so-called trivial illnesses attend regularly. The reasons for this have been discussed in the preceding chapter.
3. The assumption underlying the use of caseload as a measure of illness is that patients who are ill will take their problem to health services. As well as depending on the patients responding to their illness, this model also assumes that the health services are available to meet the patient's need. In practice access to health services varies considerably across geographical areas and for different types of illness. Thus the numbers of people being treated every year in specialized burns units partly reflects the need for such treatment, but also the availability of the units: if there are no units then, according to caseload figures, there would appear to be no need.

In practice it is almost impossible to disentangle these three phenomena; low caseload figures may reflect a healthy population, or they may reflect a shortage of health services to cope with an ill population. This means that in general caseload cannot be used as a measure of the health of a population, except in those situations when access to health services and illness behaviour patterns are believed to be the same for everyone.

● Measures of functioning

One problem with comparing the different diagnoses discovered in a community prevalence study is that different diseases cause different degrees of incapacity, and even the same disease might be found with different stages of severity. One way around this problem is to ignore the specific diagnosis and instead measure the degree of incapacity produced by the illness; in this way a case of ischaemic heart disease can be compared with a case of chronic bronchitis through finding out to what extent the disease prevents the patient from carrying out his or her normal functioning.

There are now various measures of functioning available for population surveys. They have been used particularly in surveys of chronic illness where the disease has a specific impact on daily living. For this reason these are often called activities of daily living (ADL) measures (Katz et al., 1963).

ADL measures identify certain everyday functions, sometimes divided into major and minor, which are then assessed by means of a survey. For example, major items might include such activities as feeding oneself, getting to and using a toilet, and doing up buttons and zips. Minor items might include things like putting on shoes and socks, having a bath or wash, getting in and out of bed, combing and brushing hair. Respondents would be asked whether they can do any of these items, by themselves or with help or not at all (Harris, 1971). Their responses could then be added up to create an overall score of disability. Such scores enable the amount of disability in a community to be measured and compared over time or with other communities.

A limitation of measures of function is that they rely on particular activities. But illness can affect people in many ways not only in carrying out basic everyday activities. This view has led increasingly to a strategy of asking people themselves to make their own assessments of their health status.

- ### Self-report measures

One common measure of health is simply to ask people about their self-reported acute and chronic sickness. The government General Household Survey, for example, asks a sample of people every year about their experience of acute illness in the preceding 14 days and whether they believe they have a long-standing illness. These responses can then be summed to create an overall measure of the acute illness in a population and the amount of long-standing chronic illness experienced.

Self-reported sickness is relatively easy to measure but suffers from certain serious disadvantages.

1. From the illness behaviour literature it is known that some people are more likely to take their illnesses to the doctor than others. This same bias probably also operates when reporting illness to an interviewer. Thus more 'stoical' people may minimize their degree of illness, whereas others may exaggerate it.
2. It is also known from studies in the illness behaviour area that it is not simply the readiness to report illness that varies between people but also their very perception of illness itself. Thus two people with exactly the same illness may perceive different degrees of pain, loss of energy, disability, etc.

- ### Subjective health measures

Part of the limitation of self-reported sickness is the crudity of the measure; people are simply asked whether they have had an illness or not. A different approach is to use a complete questionnaire to enquire after health status. Because such questionnaires rely on the respondents' own view of their health, such measures are called subjective health indicators. One such indicator is the Nottingham Health Profile (Hunt et al., 1986).

The Nottingham Health Profile (NHP) was developed by asking many people what they thought was important about good health. From their responses a series of questions were devised which simply require a yes/no response and take the form of 'I have pain at night', 'I find it hard to bend', 'Things are getting me down'. These different questions are then grouped into the following six categories or dimensions of health:

1. Pain
2. Physical mobility
3. Sleep
4. Energy
5. Social isolation
6. Emotional reactions

The Nottingham Health Profile has now been used on many populations, some healthy and some ill. Because it identifies different components of illness it has proved a very useful means of comparing the health of different groups of people. For example, the effects of treatments such as heart transplantation can be assessed by giving patients the NHP before and after the operation to identify the dimensions of illness in which there is improvement and the dimensions in which there is deterioration.

Medical treatments have traditionally been evaluated in terms of biological changes brought about by intervention. Thus giving iron to an anaemic woman is supposed to increase the haemoglobin level; giving antibiotics to a chest infection improves the appearance on the chest X-ray and lung function. The advantage of the NHP is that the subjective responses of the patients themselves can be added to these biological parameters.

● **Quality of life measures**
Another way of looking at health is to say that illness has an effect in terms of detracting from the quality of life. Why not, therefore, measure the quality of life directly? This can be particularly useful when assessing the value of medical intervention: a patient might not be cured but some amelioration, even if slight, of the underlying condition is often an important factor in deciding whether to use the treatment another time (Clark and Fallowfield, 1986).

There are many measures of quality of life available (Hollandsworth, 1988) though their emphases differ. Early measures tended to tap 'objective' facets of the quality of life – often defined by professional carers – whereas recent measures have tended to emphasize 'subjective' components more. The measures usually try and embrace both functional impairment and psychological wellbeing, and in this respect are often similar to a combined ADL and psychiatric morbidity score. Arguments continue as to the respective merits of different ways of measuring quality of life, but there is broad agreement that the idea of this measure is a good one in that ultimately all medical care – life-saving, curative, ameliorative, and supportive – is somehow directed towards improving the quality of life of patients.

Quality of life measures have mainly emerged in situations where it is important to evaluate 'value for money' in health service provision. They are often therefore combined with some sort of economic assessment to determine whether certain treatments are worthwhile in terms of the overall benefits they confer. For example, Quality Adjusted Life Years (QUALYs) are calculated by combining life expectancy with a measure of the expected quality of life of those years (in this case using anticipated physical mobility and freedom from pain), and then comparing the number of QUALYs achieved against the cost of different treatments (Williams, 1985).

● **Summary**
The measurement of health and illness is now a complex business and the technical issues are well discussed elsewhere (Culyer, 1983; McDowell and Newell, 1987). From the simple but crude measure of the mortality rate, it is now possible to pick up subtle changes in health status. Such evaluations are deemed to be increasingly important in evaluating medical treatments and in the provision of health care. These different measures of health also give a flavour of the wide variety of ways that health can be construed and these have significance in the examination of particular causes, patterns and effects of illness, as covered in succeeding chapters.

● **References**
Clark, A. and Fallowfield, L. J. (1986) Quality of life measurements in patients with malignant disease: a review. *Journal of the Royal Society of Medicine,* **79,** 165–169
Culyer, A. J. (ed.) (1983) *Health Indicators,* Martin Robertson, Oxford
Harris, A. I. (1971) *Handicapped and Impaired in Great Britain,* HMSO, London

Hollandsworth, J. G. (1988) Evaluating the impact of medical treatment on the quality of life: a 5-year update. *Social Science and Medicine,* **26,** 425–434

Hunt, S., McEwen, J. and McKenna, S. P. (1986) *Measuring Health Status,* Croom Helm, London

Katz, S., Ford, A. B., Moskowitz, R. W. *et al.* (1963) The index of ADL: a standardized measure of biological and psychosocial function. *Journal of the American Medical Association,* **185,** 914–919

McDowell, I. and Newell, C. (1987) *Measuring Health Status: A Guide to Rating Scales and Questionnaires,* Oxford University Press, Oxford

Williams, A. (1985) Economics of coronary artery bypass grafting. *British Medical Journal,* **291,** 326–329

4

Social causes of illness

Textbooks of pathology and of clinical medicine are replete with examples of the particular circumstances which cause disease. These traditional approaches to the causes of illness, however, have been dominated by the biomedical model which argues that a biological change is brought about by a preceding biological change. Sociology offers three challenges to this perspective:

1. The presence of many biological causes of illness is strongly influenced by social factors.
2. Because illness is multidimensional, the description of the causes of the biological lesion alone is not an adequate explanation, in that illness has psychosocial dimensions which equally need understanding.
3. There is evidence that apparently biologically-based diseases, and even death, may be directly brought about by social factors.

• Causal models

Before exploring the role of social factors in the aetiology of illness it is important to clarify the notion of cause.

The idea of causality is a complex one but it can be simply stated that if change in one variable brings about change in another, then the former can be said to cause the latter. This can be expressed in notation as:

$$A \longrightarrow B$$

where A is the cause and B the effect. Examples abound in clinical medicine: a virus causes influenza, a fall causes a fracture, atheroma causes ischaemic heart disease, etc.

But for the vast majority of diseases this model is an abstraction in that the actual causal system is known to be far more complex.

At the simplest level the supposed causal relationship between A and B ignores why A changes, and it ignores the possible 'mechanisms' by which A changes B. Thus a more comprehensive model might be:

$$x \rightarrow A \rightarrow y \rightarrow B$$

A and B are still causally related but so are x and B, and y and B. The answer to the question 'What causes B?' can now be provided in three ways, all different but all correct.

Sometimes in medicine apparently alternative explanations are merely different selections from the same causal sequence: whereas for some people, A might be held to be the cause of B, for others it is relegated to a part of the mechanisms by which x causes B. For example, it is argued later that social class is incriminated in the aetiology of various diseases such as infections and ischaemic heart disease, yet medical textbooks are more likely to stress bacteria and serum cholesterol levels. How can these two apparently different sets of explanations be reconciled?

The two explanations, the biological and the social, are not necessarily in conflict if they are taken from different points in the same causal sequence. Thus it may be that:

low $\longrightarrow$ poor $\longrightarrow$ high $\longrightarrow$ ischaemic
social class   diet   serum cholesterol   heart disease

From this causal pathway it would appear that both explanations are correct.

The picture in medicine is further complicated by the fact that disease aetiology cannot properly be represented by such a simple causal sequence; instead a multifactorial model is more appropriate:

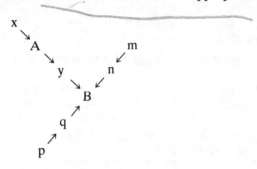

For a patient to develop tuberculosis requires both the presence of the Koch bacillus and a poor nutritional state (which might be a product of social conditions). Hence both factors may be necessary pre-conditions for developing the disease.

Thus, in medicine, when the cause of a disease is identified it represents a choice from a wide selection of possible causal factors, both in type and over time. As the environment is a factor in the causation of most diseases, and the social environment is inextricably intertwined in the biological/physical, most diseases have some social factors bound up in their aetiology as the arguments later in this chapter suggest.

● Establishing a causal relationship

There are many pitfalls in assuming that one variable causes another. These difficulties are particularly pertinent to the social sciences where it is often much harder to show a causal relationship.

There are three conditions which must be fulfilled for it to be possible to claim that two variables are causally related, e.g. A causes B (A → B).

1. They must occur in correct *temporal sequence*. The independent variable, A, must precede the dependent variable, B, in time: if it does not then their relationship cannot be causal. In the natural sciences discovering the

temporal sequence of two variables is not often a serious problem. However, in the behavioural sciences, and especially under non-experimental conditions, it may be difficult. For instance, it may be suggested that a patient became depressed as a result of losing his job, but equally plausible would be the hypothesis that he became depressed and then lost his job through an inability to work properly.

2. There must be a *correlation* between the variables such that as A varies, B varies (A $\propto$ B). Usually some statistical test will establish if a correlation exists.

3. There must be *no third explanatory variable*. This is the most difficult condition to test for. If a third variable exists which affects both A and B then the observed relationship between the latter may be spurious.

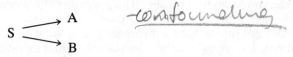

For instance, there may be a correlation between the number of television sets and heart attacks in the population:

number of television sets $\propto$ heart attacks

However, it is unlikely that one is causing the other. By introducing a third variable, affluence, a more plausible model is produced: affluence causes increased spending on consumer goods and the sale of televisions increases; at the same time affluence produces a change in life style, perhaps in diet, which may increase the heart attack rate. Thus:

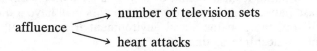

Thus the apparent relationship between numbers of television sets and heart attacks is spurious as it is explained by the third variable, affluence.

A more familiar example is that of the relationship between cigarette smoking and lung cancer. There is a well established correlation between these two variables and they occupy the correct temporal sequence (it seems highly unlikely that having lung cancer makes the patient smoke cigarettes). But is the relationship causal?

It has been suggested that it is a personality type which 'causes' both cigarette smoking and cancer. Thus it is possible to construct two different causal models to show the relationship between smoking and lung cancer.

1. smoking $\longrightarrow$ cancer

2. extraversion $\begin{array}{l} \nearrow \text{ smoking} \\ \searrow \text{ cancer} \end{array}$

In both models there is the correct temporal sequence and both models will show a correlation between smoking and cancer. A test of the latter hypothesis became available when one section of the population (doctors) radically decreased their cigarette consumption after a link between smoking and cancer was first suggested. The result was a decrease in cancer in this group. If model (2) had been correct then stopping smoking should have had no effect on their cancer rate since personalities, which supposedly cause the cancer, remained constant.

However, even though in this survey the hypothesized causal relationship between smoking and cancer was confirmed, it does not exclude other 'third' variables from being able to refute the relationship. For instance, doctors' cancer rate may have gone down not because they gave up smoking but because they also perhaps became less anxious and it is anxious people who get cancer and who tend to smoke.

In other words, the condition for causality which specifies the absence of a third variable (which shows the apparent relationship to be spurious) is unattainable. But this does not mean that the hypothesized relationship should be rejected; it is at least now known to be better than believing that extraversion causes cancer. In short the claim of causality is always a provisional one. It is only by successive testing of the relationship against the more obvious and plausible alternatives that increased reliance can be placed on the hypothesis despite its provisional nature.

• Social factors

The role of social factors in the cause of illness can be seen in two ways. There can be an indirect effect in which social factors bring the individual and a harmful physical/biological factor together in some way: for example, although it may be water-borne organisms which can cause illness it is the particular social customs of a tribe in drinking from a stream or a from a well which will help determine their disease patterns. Alternatively social factors may have a direct effect through which something in the social environment triggers an illness without any apparent physical intermediary.

Given the multifactorial aetiology of most diseases it is probable that both indirect and direct effects are involved together in many illnesses; however for purposes of description they will be dealt with separately in this chapter.

Indirect effects

The evidence for the indirect influence of social factors in bringing hazards from the physical/biological world into contact with people will be described. These influences can be seen as either general or specific.

General influence of social factors

Dubos (1980) has argued the interesting case that illness is a product of environmental maladaptation. He suggests that societies which have reached an equilibrium with their natural environment are, by and large, disease-free, disease only arising when that equilibrium is disturbed. A specific example might be the disastrous spread of European endemic infections such as measles to the immunologically unprotected populations of third world countries with the spread of colonial empires several centuries ago. But more relevant for our own society is the fact that we have changed rapidly with industrialization and continue to change; according to Dubos this continuous change produces disequilibrium and maladaptation to the environment in which we find ourselves. This in its turn produces illness. For example, if we were to stop all change in our diet or in our stress levels, then those individuals who were harmed by certain foods or stresses would have an evolutionary disadvantage and gradually, over time, their genes would be lost; the result, eventually, would be a society without diet-induced illness as everyone would be adapted to the society's foodstuffs. In other words the price of a healthy society, according to Dubos, would be one in which change, whatever its form, was replaced by stability and fixity.

Specific influence of social factors

The second and more common way of looking at the effect of the natural environment on people is to see it in terms of specific hazards. McKeown (1979) has argued that the high mortality rate in the nineteenth century – and, by implication, in third world countries today – is the product of microorganism-based diseases which flourish in a setting of insanitary conditions and poor nutrition. One of the specific examples he provides is the decline in mortality from tuberculosis, from the middle of the nineteenth century when the causes of death were first recorded, to today. Although one of the important aetiological factors in tuberculosis, the tubercle bacillus, was discovered in the late nineteenth century, it was not until 1948 that a specific treatment (streptomycin) was available. Nevertheless by 1948 over 90% of the decline in mortality from the disease had already occurred (Figure 4.1). The explanation that McKeown

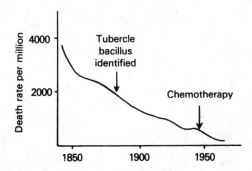

Figure 4.1. Decline in mortality from tuberculosis in England and Wales. (After McKeown, 1979)

advances for this phenomenon is the improvement in sanitation and nutrition which occurred during the nineteenth and early twentieth centuries. McKeown calculates that similar factors have been at work since the nineteenth century for most causes of death and, at the most, medical intervention (mainly since the Second World War) accounts for only about 4% of the total improvement in life expectancy.

   Although sanitary conditions in modern society have been transformed, virtually to eliminate water-borne diseases, and the nutritional state of the population has risen to such an extent that host resistance is much improved, environmental factors such as pollution, work hazards, inappropriate diet, etc. are no doubt still important factors in the aetiology of many diseases.

While each of the above environmental physical/biological factors is important in the aetiology of disease, it is important to realize that all of these factors occur in a social context. Thus, as McKeown points out, improvements in nutrition have not necessarily been consciously brought about, but reflect the improving standard of living of the population at large. Equally a brief glance at the battles fought by sanitary reformers in the nineteenth century will show that the socio-political will must also be present to introduce adequate environmental safeguards. Similarly pollution and occupational hazards relate to individual behaviour and group interests; and of course cigarette smoking, the largest cause of mortality in developed countries, is very much a behaviour which influences health.

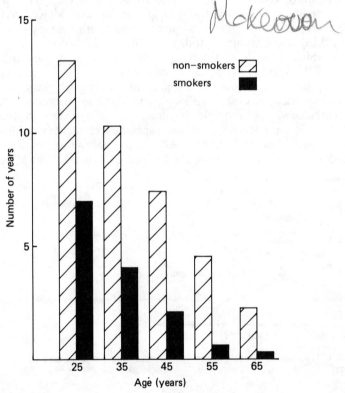

Figure 4.2. Increase in expectation of life in males from 1838–54 to 1970. (After McKeown, 1979)

McKeown provides data on the improvement in life expectancy by age group and whether smokers or not. Figure 4.2 shows that the improvement in life expectancy over the last 130 years is at least halved in each age group by the simple behaviour of smoking. Put another way, all the improvements, whether brought about by nutrition, sanitation, housing, standard of living, or medical therapeutics, is eliminated by one habit. This illustrates most powerfully the importance of belief and behaviour as risk factors in the bringing together of hazardous chemicals and the individual human body.

Direct effects

Specific environmental hazards such as cigarette smoke or unclean water can clearly damage cellular structure to such a degree as to produce clinical disease. It is, perhaps, less easy to see how a non-physical 'hazard' can bring about a similar process. Even so, at times diseases seem to arise independently of any physical factor. In addition, taking a wider notion of health which embraces subjective response and quality of life as well as physical abnormality, it is apparent that non-physical influences play a major role in ill health in our society. This has led to a theory of a general susceptibility to illness (Cassel, 1976).

Medicine often refers to such diseases as 'functional'; sometimes such illnesses have been called psychosomatic in that there appears to be a direct effect of the mind on the body. The argument can be taken a step further in that it is the social environment which both 'constructs' the mind in the socialization process and remains for the individual the source of support and meaning.

The role of non-physical hazards in the aetiology of illness is, in many ways, more difficult to show than physical insult. There are various reasons for this, and before summarizing the field it may be helpful to identify some of the problems which researchers must grapple with in attempting to establish a firm link between social factors and ill health, in whatever form.

Methodological difficulties

1. To show a relationship between say, stress and ill health, it is necessary to measure both variables, and then see if they correlate. To allow for the influence of other factors it is usual to have a control group which does not experience the threat and whose rate of illness is then compared with the experimental group. Such research designs can immediately create problems because 'natural experiments' in which a random population is stressed and a random population is not stressed, are hard to find. This means that much of this research is carried out in the laboratory, with subsequent doubts about its relevance and applicability for the world outside.
2. There are difficulties in measuring ill health which have already been outlined in Chapter 3. Mortality is relatively easy to measure, but many of the effects of psychosocial factors such as stress are believed to be forms of ill health which are less specific and definite.
3. The social factor itself must also be measured. For example, in measuring stress the researcher must decide what stress actually is. The problem is that different researchers often define it in different ways resulting in different forms of measurement and, hence, studies which are not directly comparable.
4. Finally it is often difficult to distinguish between the social factor and ill health in the measurement process. Thus a researcher trying to answer the question whether stress causes depression might ask if someone is having difficulty sleeping as an indicator of whether they are under pressure and stressed; but in addition insomnia might be used as an indicator of clinical depression. There is obviously something circular about this argument: a person with depression might well seem to be stressed if stress is measured in a similar way to that of depression.

Some of the problems often encountered in showing the effect of social influences on a person's health have been outlined to give an indication of the

Anomic · Egoistic

difficulty of the task. This means that on the one hand social science research must be very rigorous to overcome such problems, and on the other, any work completed in the area must be viewed critically by the observer. It seems ironic that some natural scientists refer to the social sciences as soft sciences; if anything, a social scientist must show more care in carrying out research or in weighing the value of studies in this area than might be expected in many natural science experiments.

The rest of this chapter will examine the notion of susceptibility in terms of the three interrelated notions of social integration, social support and life events; the next chapter looks at the other major theory of direct social aetiology, namely labelling.

● **Social integration**

Social integration played a major role in the theory of social development advanced by the great sociologist Emile Durkheim at the end of the nineteenth century (Durkheim, 1933). Durkheim argued that pre-industrial societies were characterized by such strong social integration that individualism was submerged. With the advent of industrialization and a division of labour (which divided work tasks into more and more specialized parts), the form of social integration weakened and changed. Social cohesion was now based on the cult of individuality and it was the interdependence of people which held a society together.

This shift, however, from a cohesive community based on tight social integration to a more amorphous and loosely structured society, does not necessarily go smoothly. On the one hand if social integration becomes too weak then individuals will be endangered by their isolation; on the other hand, if individual identity fails to replace community identity then the individual is said to suffer from anomie, a sort of normlessness in which identity and purpose become lost.

In a major study of suicide in the late nineteenth century in Europe, Durkheim applied his social theory to explore what might be regarded as the ultimate individual act, namely suicide (Durkheim, 1952). He argued that despite its apparent solitary nature, suicide was underpinned by fundamentally social processes. He predicted four different types of suicide (Table 4.1). In

Table 4.1 Durkheim's four types of suicide. (After Durkheim, 1952)

	Too much	Too little
Social integration	Altruistic	Egoistic
Social regulation	Fatalistic	Anomic

pre-industrial societies or in those communities in modern society which over-integrate or over-regulate their members, two forms of suicide are produced. The first is altruistic suicide in which the death results from an over-integration of the individual in the group such that concern for others overweighs personal interest: a soldier who dies for his colleagues, or a disabled member of the family who dies for his or her relatives, would be examples of

Oaks

altruistic suicide. Durkheim argued that over-regulation was relatively rare but could be found in the fatalistic suicide carried out by Indian widows in the ceremony of suti when they threw themselves on their husband's funeral pyre.

But with the break-up of traditional community and its close interpersonal ties, to be replaced by the weaker bonds of modern society, the predominant sorts of suicide become produced by under-regulation and under-integration. Thus, Durkheim argued, in modern society people mainly commit suicide because they are too isolated or because they feel their life lacks purpose and meaning.

In industrial society, in which under-integration and under-regulation are the primary hazards, any form of social bonding should, in principle, protect against suicide. Durkheim explored this possibility by examining situations in which individuals were socially isolated. For example, he reasoned from his theory that Protestants were less integrated into their religious community than Catholics and Jews and should therefore show a higher rate of suicide. Equally single people, widows and widowers, should show a higher rate than otherwise similarly positioned married people. Also he suggested that the social integration in wartime should produce lower suicide rates than peacetime. When he examined European figures for the period he found these various hypotheses confirmed by the data.

Although Durkheim's work was carried out at the turn of the century his findings and explanations for variation in suicide rates still hold today. But, more important, his insights have been extended to other forms of illness and the wider influence of poor social integration explored.

• Social support

Drawing on Durkheim's original hypotheses, modern researchers have tried to examine the relationship between social support and illness. The argument is that if social integration is weak then people will lack social support and therefore be more susceptible to illness, with the corollary that good social support will be protective.

Marriage as support

Modern suicide rates confirm, as in Durkheim's day, the value of social support insofar as single, widowed and divorced people still have higher rates than the married. Moreover it is also apparent that the single, widowed and divorced also tend to have higher mortality rates in general than married people, with some interesting specific causes of mortality (Table 4.2; Gove, 1973).

Table 4.2 Marital status and mortality. (After Gove, 1973)

	Married	*Single*	*Widowed*	*Divorced*
Mortality	1.00	1.95	2.64	3.39
Cancer of lung	1.00	1.45	2.24	3.07
Diabetes	1.00	2.69	2.46	4.32
Cirrhosis	1.00	3.29	4.61	8.84
Leukaemia	1.00	1.07	0.91	1.28

Ratios produced by dividing unmarried rate by married

These are, however, broad brush strokes. Marital status might be related to mortality rates, but there are various possible alternative explanations for this finding which do not involve a direct influence for social support.

1. Single, never married, people may start off being in general more ill – perhaps that is why they failed to marry.
2. Widowed people may have been subjected to the same environmental hazards as their spouse and therefore be more at risk for this reason.
3. Divorced people, because of their situation, may deliberately engage in hazardous activities.

Thus it may be possible to explain the link between marital status and mortality without recourse to a direct effect of social support itself. Nevertheless, as with any scientific explanation, a single cause is more elegant than proposing three different ones. The suspicion therefore remains that it is one factor, namely social support, which links together these three mortality rates in unmarried people. The search has therefore started to identify the specific links between social support and ill health.

Contacts as social support

Researchers in the area of social support have been faced with some of the methodological problems outlined above. First, what is actually meant by social support: how is it to be defined? Second, what is the best measure of ill health that is most likely to show a connection with social support?

In early studies social support was defined in terms of number of contacts. Thus, a person with ten contacts a week had twice the social support as a person with five contacts. A major long-term investigation in the USA, the Alameda County study, reported that after allowing for other known factors in the cause of death, the extent of a person's social network corresponded to their risk of early mortality (Berkman and Syme, 1979). Their measure of social network was an amalgam of various aspects of social contact and critics could argue that it was somehow constructed to fit the mortality data. Corroborative evidence however comes from another study (Schoenbach *et al.,* 1986), though in this case the size of networks seemed only linked to protection for white males.

Quality of support

The problem of measuring number of contacts as an indicator of social support is that it is possible that the actual numbers are not important. A person could have 50 contacts in a day yet none of them may be important or close enough to provide support; moreover some social ties could be a source of strain. On the other hand one close friend may be very valuable. This has led to various studies which have tried to measure the quality of contacts as well as their number (Henderson, 1980).

Support as perception

Attempts to measure the quality of supporting relationships led to the idea that perhaps 'quality' did not exist in the form of the relationship, but in the perception and expectations of the person being supported. In other words

NOT ACTUAL social support - but BELIEF in social support

friends might not actually be offering any support but if the person believes that they are – or that they would if called upon – then this should have the same psychological impact as if there was support present. In other words it was not the social support itself but the belief in the social support which was important.

If social support is simply the belief in its existence then people with strong beliefs should be more protected from illness than those without. A particular example of this is religious belief in which the person has both the perceived support of a spiritual deity and of the religious community to which they belong. Moreover religion can also be beneficial in cultivating attitudes which give the individual a helpful perspective in facing stressful situations. This latter would accord with Durkheim's observation that suicides are less common in religious groups which emphasize their sense of community. Research, however, into the effects of religious belief is made difficult by the fact that many religions often recommend certain types of behaviour which might, quite separately, be helpful or harmful to the individual.

There is limited evidence linking lowered mortality with religious affiliation, mainly because the religion is not usually placed on the death certificate in most countries. Even so, it has been shown that certain religious groups probably benefit from proscriptions on some potentially harmful behaviours. For example, Seventh Day Adventists are a religious group which abstain from alcohol, tobacco, beverages containing caffeine and from certain meats and, probably as a result, have a longer life expectancy compared with the rest of the population. Equally, Mormons are proscribed certain dietary substances, as well as smoking, and they too seem to have longer life expectancy and lower incidences of certain specific diseases. In fact it has been suggested that most of the variation observed in mortality between religious groups can be explained by cigarette smoking alone.

In studies of the effects of religion on various aspects of health and illness, it is mostly religious affiliation which has been measured and not the religious belief. Yet from the previous discussion of social support it seems that the belief – and therefore perception of support – may be important. There is some evidence to support the view that commitment to a religion, measured in terms of church attendance, does contribute to better health (Hannay, 1980). However, there may be selective effects such that those who feel ill do not participate as extensively in religious activities as those who feel well.

Other studies also suggest an important influence of religious commitment on social support and health. The Alameda County study (Berkman and Syme, 1979) showed that church attendance was related to low mortality, though church attendance was simply one component of a wider social network. Another study (Kasl and Ostfield, 1984) examined 400 elderly poor for their religiousness and mortality. They found that church attendance and self-rated religiousness both seemed to have an effect on decreasing mortality which suggests that the effect of religion was probably not only due to social contacts.

The idea that social support might protect people from illness and death remains a fascinating one and despite the measurement difficulties the number of investigations in the field is expanding rapidly.

● **Life events**

It has been observed over many years that a negative life event such as bereavement is likely to precipitate a reaction which resembles clinical depression. This has led researchers to suggest that negative life events, like the loss of a bereavement, may be important in the aetiology of other diseases.

Early attempts to measure life events used a checklist format in which respondents had simply to tick if any particular event had happened to them in a certain time period (Holmes and Rahe, 1967). These events were then weighted by the researchers according to their assessment of severity, and the resulting values summed to give an overall life event score. In recent years researchers have argued that this technique is too crude because it fails to take into account the particular meanings of events for different people. For example, for most people the death of a spouse is a very negative and traumatic event, but for some it may be a release from a very strained and difficult situation. In other words it is important to know the context of the event before rating its degree of threat for the individual. A common procedure now is to tape record a semi-structured interview (that is one which is conducted more like a conversation) with a respondent in which both events and their meaning are discussed, and then later, while listening to the tape, assess the significance of any event for that particular person.

Most work on the influence of life events in the aetiology of disease has concentrated on psychiatric disorder (Dohrenwend and Dohrenwend, 1981). While it was known that the death of a close friend or relative produced a bereavement reaction with close similarities to depression, the bereavement reaction was believed to be a normal event which tended to be self-limiting. But depression was a clinical syndrome which continued beyond a reasonable time and, indeed, in many cases did not seem to be preceded by life events. Early work therefore concentrated on identifying to what extent all depressive episodes could be related to external negative life events.

Brown and his co-workers carried out an in-depth study of women in south London to relate life events to depressive disorder (Brown and Harris, 1978). They found a fairly clear relationship between experiencing a life event and the onset of a depressive disorder, though the influence of the life event on the illness also seemed to depend on several other 'vulnerability' factors which might increase the susceptibility of the women in the study to becoming depressed. These factors were: no employment outside the home, the presence of children under five at home, lack of a good intimate relationship with someone, and the loss of the woman's own mother before the age of 11. The model they proposed was therefore multifactorial, but it meant that if the vulnerability risk factors were all against a woman then a life event became much more likely to tip her into depression. For example, for working class women with young children at home in a poor marriage, the risk of clinical depression was almost 50%. Much of the depression brought about by life events, of course, following on the knowledge of illness behaviour, was unknown to health services either psychiatric or general practitioner.

In an extension to the south London study, Brown and his co-workers looked at the prevalence of psychiatric disorder on the Hebridean island of North Uist (Brown et al., 1977). They found that while the overall amount of psychiatric morbidity on the island was not dissimilar to that found in the London study, the type of illness was different. Whereas in London almost all the morbidity had been depression, on North Uist there was a sizeable amount of anxiety as well. (Most depressive disorder has anxiety components and vice versa; however in most cases a major component can be identified.)

resonate

The interesting feature of the distribution of depression and anxiety in North Uist was its relationship to social integration. Thus those women who were closely integrated into the traditional community on the island (those born on the island, working in traditional industries, and being closely linked to the church) were more likely to suffer from anxiety whereas the others, like the Camberwell women, were more likely to suffer from depression. This finding resonates with Durkheim's original observations of the protective features of social integration and social support. Brown speculates that the integrated women were only experiencing psychiatric disorder because their traditional way of life was changing rapidly with the new oil industry and developing tourism. This made their traditional security seem precarious and produced an anxiety reaction in the women.

There have since been several attempts to establish a link between life events and organic disease (Creed, 1985). There seems to be some support for an influence of life events on subarachnoid haemorrhage, myocardial infarction and functional abdominal pain. One study which did show an interesting link between abdominal pain and life events involved patients with appendicitis presenting at a Manchester hospital (Creed, 1981). All the patients in the sample were asked about preceding life events; these events were grouped into two types, threatening and severe. Pathology reports on the removed appendix were then examined. These showed, as is usual, that about half the appendices removed were not pathologically inflamed. But when the pathology report was related to the experience of life events it was found that those patients with severe events were more likely to have a non-inflamed appendix whereas those patients with inflamed appendices were more likely to have experienced a threatening event.

It is clear that life events and social support are related, but there is some debate as to the connection. One view is that social support has an influence on illness quite independent of life events, though often the two can be additive. The other view is that social support offers a 'buffer' for life events in which the negative impact of an event is somehow reduced by good social support. For example, a study of social support in physically disabled people found that low social support was associated with significant deterioration in psychosocial and emotional functioning only in the presence of adverse life events (Patrick *et al.*, 1986). Many studies have now shown the value of careful methodological work in the elucidation of the role of life events in illness. Debates continue as to the best method of measuring life events and their precise relationship with social support, but the area promises to be an interesting one.

● **References**

Berkman, L. F. and Syme, S. L. (1979) Social networks, host resistance, and mortality: a nine year follow-up study of Alameda County residents. *American Journal of Epidemiology,* **109**, 186–204

Brown, G. W. and Harris, T. (1978) *Social Origins of Depression: A Study of Psychiatric Disorder in Women,* Tavistock, London

Brown, G. W., Davidson, S., Harris, T. *et al.* (1977) Psychiatric disorder in London and North Uist. *Social Science and Medicine,* **11**, 367–377

Cassel, J. (1976) The contribution of the social environment to host resistance. *American Journal of Epidemiology,* **104**, 107–123

Creed, F. (1981) Life events and appendicectomy. *Lancet,* **i**, 1381–1385

Creed, F. (1985) Life events and physical illness: a review. *Journal of Psychosomatic Research,* **29**, 113–124

Dohrenwend, B. S. and Dohrenwend, B. P. (eds) (1981) *Stressful Life Events and their Context,* Produst, New York

Dubos, R. (1980) *Man Adapting,* Yale University Press, New Haven

Durkheim, E. (tr. 1933) *The Division of Labour in Society,* Macmillan, New York

Durkheim, E. (1952) *Suicide: A Study in Sociology,* Routledge and Kegan Paul, London

Gove, W. R. (1973) Sex, marital status and mortality. *American Journal of Sociology,* **79**, 45–67

Hannay, D. R. (1980) Religion and health. *Social Science and Medicine,* **14a**, 683–685

Henderson, S. A. (1980) A development in social psychiatry: the systematic study of social bonds. *Journal of Nervous and Mental Diseases,* **168**, 63–69

Holmes, T. H. and Rahe, R. H. (1967) The social readjustment rating scale. *Journal of Psychosocial Research,* **11**, 213–218

Kasl, F. V. and Ostfield, A. N. (1984) Psychosocial predictors of mortality among the elderly poor: the role of religion, well-being and social contact. *American Journal of Epidemiology,* **119**, 410–423

McKeown, T. (1979) *The Role of Medicine,* Blackwell, Oxford

Patrick, D. L., Morgan, M. and Charlton, R. H. (1986) Psychosocial support and change in the health status of physically disabled people. *Social Science and Medicine,* **22**, 1347–1354

Schoenbach, V. J., Kaplan, B. H., Fredman, L. *et al.* (1986) Social ties and mortality in Evans County, Georgia. *American Journal of Epidemiology,* **123**, 577–591

5

Labelling behaviour

One of the theories of how life events have their impact on people is through self-esteem. Day-to-day interaction can be looked upon as requiring so much self-esteem, but when that self-esteem is jeopardized, such as by a life event, then people are unable to cope and manifest signs of psychological disturbance. One other mechanism by which self-esteem might be disturbed is that of labelling.

Labelling refers to the process whereby individual characteristics are identified by others and given a negative label (Lemert, 1967). This label may be accepted by the person and as a result produce behaviour changes in conformity with the label. The process by which some characteristics of a person are labelled negatively involves judgements being made of what is socially normal or acceptable and what is socially abnormal or deviant.

The height of someone taken from the tail of a normal population distribution is 'abnormal' to the extent that it, say, lies outside two standard deviations of the mean, but it is only 'deviant' if it is in some way held to be socially abnormal. Startlingly blue eyes may be remarked upon as unusual but the person is unlikely to be cast as deviant, unlike perhaps the albino whose eye colour is both unusual and socially strange. Deviance therefore implies some degree of negative social evaluation.

But why is it that of two unusual eye colours one is deviant and the other is not? Why is it that a man who talks to himself in church is praying, while a man who talks to himself in the street is mad? 'Labelling theory', as it is often called, has been developed to help answer these questions. It is divided between two notions of deviance, primary and secondary.

- **Primary deviance**

The concept of primary deviance relates to the actual defining of a state or behaviour as 'deviant'. Thus the act of diagnosis, of affixing disease labels to people, is a process of classification by which people are labelled ill (deviant) or healthy.

Labelling as a means of creating diseases must be distinguished from the cause of diseases. The cause of someone being ill or healthy is to be found in the preceding events which had as their consequence the particular state of illness or health. Both 'abnormal' pathology and 'normal' physiology are biological states for which there may be identifiable biological causes, but whether the biological state is a disease or not is established by the decision of the doctor when the diagnosis or label is affixed to the patient.

The labelling of primary deviance is important because it enables apparently similar phenomena to be separated into socially acceptable and unacceptable. A gang of working class teenagers who break windows in a public building might be labelled as 'vandals', but a group of drunken medical students after a rugby game carrying out a similar act might be more likely to be showing 'high spirits'. Similarly if a person claims with some conviction that he is Napoleon, it might be considered good acting if he is on the stage or schizophrenia if he is in the doctor's surgery. Again the behaviour in both instances may be virtually the same but the social interpretation – and therefore the label – differs.

The labelling of primary deviance is therefore a means by which the normal is reaffirmed and the deviant is identified. Labelling in this sense serves to delineate the boundaries of what is considered to be normal social values and behaviour (Becker, 1963). From this perspective diagnosis is a process of identifying and labelling primary deviance which defines the bounds of social normality, especially in that disease categories themselves embody such evaluations (see Chapter 13).

● Secondary deviance

Secondary deviance refers to the change in behaviour that occurs as a consequence of labelling. Strong social pressures tend to promote behaviour in conformity with the label and labelling thereby becoming a 'self-fulfilling prophecy' (Schur, 1971).

Stereotyping

The pressures on patients to change their behaviour arise from the social meaning and significance of the label the doctor has applied. A blind person may be seen as quiet and docile, a psychiatric patient as mad, an epileptic as violent. These particular stereotypes may affect both patients' perception of themselves and the responses of friends and relatives to them.

Interpersonal interaction

The interpersonal behaviour of a labelled person may be affected as people around them respond differently. This response, whether it is based on an attempt to ignore or help the patient, can reaffirm the new self-image of the labelled person. Do people talk to the blind person on the bus in the same way that they talk with other people? Some people can become quite embarrassed when they suddenly discover that the person they were talking to at the table is paraplegic: what had they been saying? Had they inadvertently said things which may have shocked or hurt?

The response of so-called normal people to disability, for example, may be well-meaning but the result can often be to bring the behaviour of the person so labelled into conformity with people's expectations. There is some evidence, for example, of a 'halo' effect in the classroom such that if a teacher is told that certain children are intelligent, even if they are only of medium ability, the labelled children achieve better results than children of seemingly similar ability.

Retrospective interpretation

The other means by which behaviour towards so-called deviant people, particularly the mentally ill, differs is that it often goes back into their past life to find events and behaviour which will make today's label seem a reasonable judgement. This process of 'retrospective interpretation' occurs in everyday interaction and is also commonly found in the media coverage of events. The suicide of an apparently contented public figure seems perplexing until past events, perhaps a bout of depression five years ago, make sense of the event. But does it? Most of the people who have bouts of depression during the past five years do not commit suicide. And what of the last four years of contentment? Why does a depressive episode of a few months' duration several years ago matter more than the recent mood? The answer is that the present is comprehended and interpreted by reference to the past – if necessary distorting the past to make it justify the present.

In many ways a doctor's notes are distortions of past events because they are selective. They do not record when the patient did not have headaches or was very happy, only when the headaches occurred or when the depressive bouts erupted. This is not to argue that the current basis of writing case notes is wrong, only to point out that one of the unintended consequences of this practice may be to reinforce in the doctor's mind the correctness of the current diagnosis.

i.e. only put what is WRONG in notes not what is RIGHT.

Relevance of secondary deviance to medicine

The notion of secondary deviance is of importance to medicine in that certain disease labels carry with them public stereotypes which may change a patient's behaviour. Thus a man fully recovered from a myocardial infarction may refuse to return to work and become a near invalid who is confined to the house because of the image he and his family and friends have of the 'coronary cripple'. A diagnosed epileptic may refuse to climb stairs, go swimming or cross a busy road and may become depressed and withdrawn, again because of the social meaning placed on the diagnostic label.

In many cases these consequences are almost unavoidable; it is only by giving the patient a diagnosis, whether it is blindness, epilepsy, sexually transmitted disease, etc. that adequate treatment and care can be arranged for the patient. In other cases the effect can be lessened if the doctor is aware of the potential effects the diagnosis might carry and therefore handles it more cautiously. In other words a diagnosis is not simply a convenient classification given to some underlying biological phenomenon: it may also be a label which carries significant social meaning. To tell a patient he has Hashimoto's disease will probably draw a blank, but to tell a patient he is blind, a diabetic or an epileptic may well set in motion significant changes in his life as a direct consequence of the social meaning carried by the diagnosis (Scott, 1969). In the end these changes may have a greater effect on the patient's life than the biological dysfunction which was originally described.

● Stigma

The power of a label to bring about secondary deviance stems from social reaction to the person so labelled. In part it is the patient's own reaction to the label; but this only occurs because the label itself carries a meaning which is sustained by a more general social reaction. Thus, the patient reacts to a diagnosis of 'heart disease' because of the more general social interpretation of the meaning of the problem.

For certain health problems, however, it is not the medical diagnosis which evinces the social reaction but the general visibility of the particular condition. A patient who cannot see or hear or walk can easily be socially identified without a formal medical diagnosis; and because they obviously do not possess all of the attributes of 'normal' people they may be seen in some sense as socially unacceptable or inferior. People with such 'abnormalities' are said to be *stigmatized* (Goffman, 1963).

People with stigmatized conditions are essentially outsiders: their stigma marks them out for social rejection. However in terms of the impact of a label on the person it is not only the social reaction which is important, but also the imagined social reaction. Thus many patients with epilepsy successfully conceal it from friends and relatives (and even their spouses) so there is no overt social reaction to the diagnosis; however these patients can still experience 'felt stigma' in that they feel themselves as being inferior, as hiding a discreditable part of their character from the world outside (Scambler and Hopkins, 1986).

When the stigma is more overt there is less opportunity to 'pass' as normal. In these circumstances many stigmatized people form their own alternative communities or clubs in which, through meeting people with similar afflictions, they can feel relatively normal and accepted. Yet, while forming an outside group may help their sense of social isolation, this can further remove and alienate them from so-called normal society. Stigma therefore produces a dilemma for the patient: on the one hand they can attempt to be part of normal society, yet they will be constantly reminded that they are not 'normal' and risk discovery at any time; on the other hand they can establish their own 'normal' society of similar outsiders which further alienates them from the bulk of the population.

In part the response of those stigmatized will be determined by the visibility and obtrusiveness of their stigma. Patients with colostomies (which require the passing of the contents of their colon through a hole in their abdominal wall into a plastic bag worn under their clothing) usually pass as normal, although this might require changes in lifestyle and occasional social embarrassment. Patients with major sensory deficits are more likely to form their own subgroups but such groups, as pointed out above, can lead to tensions. Thus, for example, deaf people can communicate by either lip reading or using hand signs, but because one method tends to dominate they can be classified either as readers or signers. Readers are obviously better able to cope in a hearing world yet signers are able, through their more exclusive language, to feel more united as a group (Higgins, 1980). Indeed even within the world of the deaf, readers who can attempt to pass as not deaf can be stigmatized by signers whose primary identity is based on being deaf, because they are not committed members of the deaf community.

The dilemma for the stigmatized of choosing whether to be abnormal in a normal world or normal in an abnormal world is also reflected in social and health policy. Mentally subnormal children can be educated in a normal school where they will be marked out as abnormal or they go to a special school where, though their abnormality will not be marked, they will be further removed from normal society. The deaf can be taught lipreading to enable them to integrate as best they can, or they can be taught sign language to enable them to gain an identity through segregation; the stigmatized can often make the choice themselves, although because of their organization, commitment and rejection of trying to integrate, it is often those in favour of segregation whose views are heard.

For the patient the management of stigma is a difficult and never-ending task and while doctors, nurses and other health professionals might not be able to remove the stigma nor advise the patient on how best they should run their own lives, there are undoubtedly many occasions when sympathetic counselling and support of the patient may be of considerable help (see Chapter 8).

● Disability and handicap

The fact that the social reaction to impairment or disability can be just as important for the person so labelled as the original biological deficit has been recognized in a model which incorporates the social reaction (Figure 5.1; WHO, Figure 5.1, 1980).

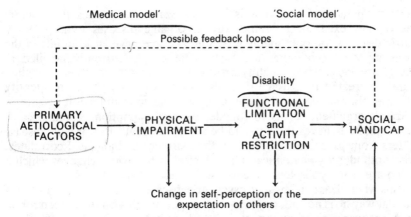

Figure 5.1. Model of impairment, disability and handicap. (After WHO, 1980)

The traditional 'medical model' encompasses the specific *physical impairment* and its preceding causes if these are known. This physical impairment has two consequences: first it leads to *functional limitation* and *activity restriction* which might together be labelled as *disability*. Second, through the changes in self-perception and expectation of others (often through stigma) it creates *social handicap* which in its turn may affect and exacerbate the underlying physical impairment.

Use of this model can enable the separate dimensions of the patient's problem to be identified and appropriate management instituted. In addition, it helps in understanding the measurement of the extent of these problems.

● Labelling and psychiatric disease

Secondary deviance has been extensively used to analyse psychiatry (Ingleby, 1981). This is probably for three reasons:

1. Psychiatric diagnosis is less precise than diagnosis in the rest of medicine with the result that it is easier for the critic to dispute the existence, type or natural history of psychiatric disorders.
2. Unlike most organic diagnoses, psychiatric conditions carry much greater social significance. Madness for centuries has been the basis of many and varied social theories and practices.
3. The manifestations of mental illness are principally in changed behaviour, and as labelling too may lead to altered behaviour, it may be difficult to distinguish the relative effects of the mental illness itself from the effects of the labelling.

The importance given to the effects of labelling in psychiatry varies from psychiatrist to psychiatrist. Most would now acknowledge its value in explaining some psychiatric problems; some go so far as to suggest that it can explain all psychiatric morbidity. Three types of argument can be identified.

Psychiatric illness is a consequence of the labelling of primary deviance

The main proponent of this view is Thomas Szasz who argues that mental diseases do not exist in the same way as organic diseases (Szasz, 1962). Psychiatric diseases are only metaphors: some people have 'sick' minds in the same way as some economies are 'sick'. The people currently labelled as mentally ill are those whose slightly incongruous behaviour has been labelled and therefore treated by psychiatrists. Psychiatrists do not therefore identify 'real' disease, they simply label 'inappropriate' behaviour and call it disease.

Szasz's argument seems to founder on his assumptions about organic disease in that he believes the latter to be somehow 'real'. But organic disease only differs from psychiatric disorder in the existence of biological correlates; otherwise both identify anatomical, physiological or behaviour changes which it is believed are socially disadvantageous (see Chapter 14).

Thus when Szasz claims that psychiatric disease only 'exists' because it is labelled that way he is not offering a special insight, for this can be argued for all disease. Moreover such an argument does little to help people who suffer from 'psychiatric phenomena', whatever their status, and it fails to appreciate the way in which social phenomena can have 'real' effects on people's lives.

Psychiatric illness is a consequence of the labelling of primary deviance and the resulting secondary deviance

This view holds that psychiatrists identify a behaviour pattern which, though it may be slightly unusual, is still within the normal range, label it as psychiatric disease (i.e. primary deviance) and by a process of investigation and treatment induce the mental illness that was first labelled (i.e. by secondary deviance). The power of this argument stems from two factors:

1. The supposed unsettling impact for someone who is told they are or might be mentally ill (patients are still often referred to the 'nerve doctor' because of the negative social evaluation placed on many aspects of psychiatric illness).
2. The investigation and treatment environment places the patient in an abnormal situation in which the 'correct' behaviour is difficult to establish. On the one hand 'normal' behaviour is clearly abnormal in a mental hospital,

and on the other hand abnormal behaviour merely fulfills the psychiatrist's predictions.

An experiment conducted in a State hospital in the USA illustrates the argument (Rosenhan, 1973). The researcher and his co-workers all managed to get themselves admitted by reporting hallucinations the night before. Thereafter they behaved completely normally and it took an average of 30 days to get discharged. Behaviour which was normal for the researchers (taking notes) was viewed by the staff as bizarre: it was described in the day-book as 'engaged in writing behaviour'. The 'patients' who were discharged earliest were those who eventually confessed to having been ill but were now 'feeling better'. Those who continued to profess their normality were kept in the longest as it was believed they were deliberately feigning to get out – clearly pathological behaviour in a mental hospital. (The only people within the hospital to realize the researchers were 'normal' were the other patients!)

Though this study demonstrated the dilemma of appropriate behaviour in a mental hospital it is uncertain whether it substantiates the labelling perspective. One critic has argued it merely shows the diagnostic ineptitude of the admitting psychiatrists. This is probably the significant point. It is only when early mistakes are made in diagnosis that 'normal' patients are exposed to the potentially unsettling experience of being a patient in a psychiatric setting. Yet it can be argued that because psychiatric diagnostic categories are relatively imprecise, mistakes can be made. Occasionally a mistake is brought to light by the media but it is impossible without further empirical study to judge the overall impact of this process on the emergence of new psychiatric cases.

Psychiatric illness can be exacerbated by labelling and secondary deviance

The evidence to support this hypothesis comes from patients who have been incarcerated for long periods of time in mental hospitals. They manifest behaviour which is appropriate for the inside of a mental hospital but which is incongruous for the world outside. This phenomenon of institutionalization denotes the process by which the inmates of large institutions gradually withdraw from normal life and become wholly dependent (Goffman, 1961).

There is now general awareness of the dangers of prolonged institutionalization and some of these effects can be combated by minimizing the period of hospitalization and, where hospitalization is necessary, by ensuring a suitable ward environment (Jones and Fowles, 1984). One effect of 'therapeutic communities' which reject traditional ward structure and authority is to prepare the patient for rapid integration back into the community when sufficiently recovered.

● **References**

Becker, H. S. (1963) *Outsiders: Studies in the Sociology of Deviance,* Free Press, London

Goffman, E. (1961) *Asylums,* Penguin, London

Goffman, E. (1963) *Stigma: Notes on the Management of Spoiled Identity,* Penguin, London

Higgins, P. C. (1980) *Outsiders in a Hearing World: A Sociology of Deafness,* Sage, London

Ingleby, D. (ed.) (1981) *Critical Psychiatry: The Politics of Mental Health,* Penguin, London

Jones, K. and Fowles, A. J. (1984) *Ideas on Institutions,* Routledge and Kegan Paul, London

Lemert, E. (1967) *Human Deviance, Social Problems and Social Control,* Prentice Hall, Hemel Hempstead

Rosenhan, D. (1973) On being sane in insane places. *Science,* **179**, 250–258

Scambler, G. and Hopkins, A. (1986) Being epileptic: coming to terms with stigma. *Sociology of Health and Illness,* **8**, 26–43

Schur, E. (1971) *Labelling Deviant Behaviour,* Harper and Row, London

Scott, R. A. (1969) *The Making of Blind Men,* Russell Sage, London

Szasz, T. S. (1962) *The Myth of Mental Illness,* Paladin, St Albans

WHO (1980) *International Classification of Impairments, Disabilities and Handicaps,* WHO, Geneva

6

Social patterns of illness: I

In any population, at any point in time, there will be a variety of different illnesses. These illnesses often form patterns because of some biological characteristic of the disease process. For example, influenza epidemics usually show temporal patterns, being more common during winter months, and also geographical patterns as the virus is passed from one person to another through the community. Such patterns are of particular interest because:

1. They can often be used to identify the disease or its characteristics.
2. They can suggest its causal factors.
3. They can indicate areas of health need which may require targeting by the health care services.

● Explaining illness patterns

The value of looking for patterns of illness is that if the distribution of a disease and a population characteristic (e.g. age, sex, height, blood group, religion, etc.) are similar then it suggests that the characteristic is a possible aetiological factor in the disease. For example, to take a hypothetical case, if the distribution of tall men in the community was similar to the distribution of asthma (i.e. asthma was found to be more common in tall men than short) then the suspicion would emerge that tallness was possibly somehow a contributory cause of asthma.

However the observed correlation (where there is tallness there is also asthma) might also be explained in other ways:

1. The causal relationship is in fact the other way round, that asthma in men caused them to grow taller. (Chapter 4 discussed the importance of a knowledge of the temporal order of the variables before imputing causality.)
2. Something else, say an unknown hormone, causes tallness and asthma, so the two are not causally related at all. (Again, from Chapter 4, the requirement that the relationship is not spurious in deciding causality.)
3. The observed relationship is an artefact of the measuring process: perhaps the criteria for diagnosing asthma have not been adjusted to take account of the different lung function of tall people so that they seem, mistakenly, to have a higher rate of the disease.

Any similarities between the distribution of illness and other factors need to be treated cautiously: on the one hand patterns of illness can illustrate important aspects of the illness, but on the other it is all too easy to draw false conclusions. The rest of this chapter and the next will therefore describe known relationships between illness and social groupings, and then offer an evaluation of possible alternative hypotheses.

● Historical changes

Nineteenth century

With the advent of the registration of all deaths in the nineteenth century it became possible to look for patterns in both the distribution of deaths and in their specific causes. Three main configurations of illness stood out in these early studies:

1. First was the evidence that the death rate varied between different parts of the country. In part this was a product of the movement of infectious epidemics through the community, but also nineteenth century epidemiologists noted that mortality rates varied by whether the area was urban or rural. They explained the difference in terms of environmental hazards, particularly those caused by poor sanitation.
2. With detailed mortality statistics, the nineteenth century epidemiologist was able to confirm that mortality and many causes of death were closely related to age. The first few years of life were found to be dangerous for the infant; thereafter mortality declined before it began its upward climb from middle age.
3. In similar fashion, there seemed to be particular risks for males such as higher infant and occupational mortality as well as an overall shorter life expectancy.

Twentieth century

The three main nineteenth century patterns of death, namely geography, age and sex, have remained of importance in the twentieth century, but other aspects of the patterning of illness have also achieved prominence:

1. The major nineteenth century patterns of disease distribution, namely geography, age and sex, which had been viewed solely as manifestations of biological and physical influences, both within the body and in the environment, have increasingly been linked to psychosocial factors.
2. As well as being related to mortality, geography, age and sex are also correlated with many other aspects of people's lives, which in their turn have suggested more complex factors in the aetiology of disease and cause of death. Thus, while mortality was linked to the urban/rural environment, so was poverty; and while the patient's gender determined their life expectancy it also affected a whole range of other life opportunities. Therefore, by comparing the distribution of mortality with the distribution of other community characteristics it became possible to look for other relationships which may have aetiological significance.
3. New measures of ill health, as described in Chapter 3, have enabled more subtle illness patterns to be identified.

When the nineteenth century epidemiologists examined age and sex and their relationship to mortality they were dividing the population into two forms of category: these were strata and non-strata. Age is a stratified variable. In other words it represents a scale on which people can be placed, with the implication that one end of the scale has 'more' of the characteristic than the other. Thus age might be given in terms of years, or it might be given in terms of age groups or cohorts. Gender, on the other hand, is not stratified, it being impossible to rank males and females. The rest of this chapter examines some non-stratified social patterns which seem to relate to illness; the next chapter deals with stratified patterns.

● Geography

As in the nineteenth century, there are geographical differences in health status. For example, in terms of mortality the north of the UK has worse health than the south. Four hypotheses have been advanced to explain this phenomenon:

1. The finding is an artefact. More working class people live in the north than in the south and the former have higher mortality (see next chapter): therefore it is not the region which contributes to higher mortality but the particular social class mix in it.
2. The environmental and occupational hazards in the north are greater and these together produce a higher mortality.
3. There has been a long-term 'drift' of healthier people from the north to the south so affecting the age/sex standardized mortality rate (Bentham, 1988).
4. The poorer health care facilities in the north mean that there are more preventable deaths than in the south.

There is evidence that geographical health differences are not entirely caused by the social class mix as geographical variations exist even within particular social classes. Otherwise it would appear most likely that the explanation for geographical variation is a combination of the other three explanations.

● Occupation

Occupational hazards no doubt still play a part in mortality differences. The Registrar General is able to look at the various causes of mortality by occupational group and identify those diseases which are found to excess in certain occupations. Examples of these are given in Table 6.1.

Table 6.1 Occupational mortality. (After OPCS, 1978)

Occupation	Disease with excess mortality	Standardized mortality ratio
Ceramic workers	Influenza	780
Steel erectors	Accidental falls	1401
Clerks	Chronic rheumatic heart disease	143
Electronic engineers	Asthma	561
Doctors	Liver cirrhosis	311
Textile labourers	Duodenal ulcer	367
Maintenance fitters	Cancer of colon	152

All significant: $P < 0.01$

Some causes of death are self-explanatory: steel erectors die more frequently from accidental falls, whilst doctors die more frequently from alcohol-induced liver cirrhosis. Yet others are probably artefacts of the measuring process: clerical workers who die from chronic rheumatic heart disease probably had the disease before they took their occupation. Yet others are rather perplexing. Why ceramic workers should die more frequently from influenza or maintenance fitters from carcinoma of the colon is unknown. The full list of occupations with their different excess mortalities is a relatively unexplored source of ideas about the aetiology of many diseases.

●   Gender

There are two major gender differences in health status in our society which seem to be contradictory.

1. The mortality experience of men is far worse than women, women living on average about seven years longer than men. This suggests that maleness is a high risk factor for ill health.
2. The morbidity of women seems to be higher than that of men. Measuring morbidity is difficult (see Chapter 3), but according to at least three measures, namely surveys of self-reported illness, data on using health services (which is probably an acceptable indicator given that availability of services is relatively constant in any comparison between the sexes), and some morbidity surveys, women have more illnesses than men.

In summary, women get ill but men die. How is this apparent contradiction to be explained? First it is important to stress that the explanation is likely to be a social one. There are some diseases which are linked to sex chromosomes and some, such as gynaecological disorders, which are specific to biological sex differences, but most diseases occur in both men and women. Even a possible protective hormonal balance for women is challenged by the continuation of preferential survival after the menopause. In addition there is cross-cultural evidence of different patterns of disease between the sexes (in which it is the men who seem to get more illnesses and women who have shorter life expectancy) which also challenges the view that their diseases are biologically fixed.

This leaves various possible explanations for the higher illness rate in women and higher mortality rate in men. One possibility of this contradiction is that the types of illnesses suffered by men and women are different. Diseases which cause death are different from the diseases which cause non-fatal illnesses; men may have more of the former and women more of the latter. But why should this be so?

Some of the apparent excess morbidity amongst women may be a product of a related lowered illness threshold and greater propensity to report illness either in health surveys or in terms of visiting the doctor (see Chapter 2) (Nathanson, 1977). Even so, it can be argued that this increased reporting of illness is itself part of the same problem, namely a greater awareness of poorer health.

It has been argued that the diseases which cause death, in particular heart disease and cancer, are closely linked with male lifestyle in our society. Men seem to be more competitive, aggressive and rushed: they therefore are more likely to indulge in health-harming activities – smoking, alcohol, bad diet, etc. –

as a coping response, and this, combined with the direct effect of these stressors, leads to a higher incidence of fatal diseases (Waldron, 1976).

Women on the other hand have different sorts of stressors. Their traditional role is more passive and dependent, and their subsidiary social position often engenders low self-esteem. Taken together these aspects of women's social position may produce many minor illnesses, particularly psychiatric. If women had the same occupational and social environments as men – which can be examined by comparing men and women in similar jobs and circumstances – then their rate of minor psychiatric disturbance is no worse than that of men (Jenkins, 1985). However it is not simply a question of having paid jobs if domestic responsibilities remain a major part of a woman's role. Women in paid employment do seem to have better health, but only if over 40 years of age or without children; young mothers with full-time work have worse health unless they have access to adequate resources to help cope with their multiple roles (Arber et al., 1985).

Neither of these gender roles is fixed – nor necessarily acceptable. Male lifestyle which produces high mortality needs examining; women's lifestyle which produces feelings of illness also needs addressing. In part the women's movement of the last few decades has played an important role in identifying gender differences, but it is not simply a case of female emancipation in the labour force, because if followed through this would produce female mortality rates to rival those of men. Some indication of the latter may be seen in the rising prevalence of smoking amongst women and the subsequent increase in heart disease and lung cancer which is beginning to make its appearance (Wells, 1987).

• Ethnicity

Various differences in illnesses have been reported among ethnic groups in the population. While there are some very broad patterns to the distribution of these illnesses – higher rates of ischaemic heart disease amongst Asians, greater prevalence of strokes and hypertension among Afro-Caribbeans – the remarkable feature of these illnesses is the marked variation within the non-white community. This represents the different indirect and direct effect of social factors in the aetiology of illness, as each ethnic group pursues its different lifestyle. Given that there are several hundred different ethnic groups identifiable in the population it is impractical to cover their health and risk factor differences, even if these were known in any detail.

Some ethnic variability in illness is a product of particular inherited disorders such as sickle cell and thalassaemia, but the major part further confirms the different ways in which social factors influence health. Material factors are clearly important, e.g. diet is important in rickets and probably tuberculosis; others are determined by cultural patterns (Donovan, 1984). It is unclear what role cultural patterns have in the higher rates of mental disorder reported among the black community. In part, it may be a response to a lifetime of discrimination, in all its forms, but also it is possible that some behaviour patterns more frequently found in certain ethnic cultures may become labelled as psychiatric illness (Littlewood and Lipsedge, 1981).

By and large the mortality experience of immigrants is better than the host community, suggesting that healthier than average individuals 'selected' themselves for immigration (Marmot et al., 1984). In addition, the social ties which immigrants bring and maintain in their host country may have an influence on their patterns of illness (Marmot and Syme, 1976).

• Unemployment

Economic retrenchment in many Western countries over the last decade has produced higher rates of unemployment than at any time since the inter-war depression. There is evidence, particularly from studies of unemployed men, that their mortality and illness is greater than those in employment.

The effects of unemployment can be divided into psychological and material. For a minority unemployment will be welcomed. They may have sufficient income from redundancy money, pension, and state benefits, etc. yet be released from what might be a noisy and hazardous work environment. In addition leaving certain forms of work behind may reduce stress and give an opportunity to engage in valued activities. In such cases it might be expected that unemployment would produce beneficial effects on health.

However, for the vast majority unemployment forms a major life crisis. There is a fall in income which will affect the material resources available to the unemployed and their family. Secondly, there are major psychological changes: the unemployed person suffers loss of role and way of life; there is a loss of social contacts which were maintained through work; there is loss of self-esteem; and there is anxiety about the future and feelings of rejection. Many of these harmful health effects may in addition extend to the families of the unemployed.

Taken together these various observations about the experience of unemployment would suggest that it is likely that unemployed people would experience more illness. In fact the evidence from mortality figures and from morbidity surveys do indeed show worse health amongst the unemployed (Moser *et al.*, 1987; Arber, 1987).

However, before the observed correlation between illness and unemployment can be taken as evidence that unemployment causes illness, it is necessary to consider two alternative explanations.

1. It is possible that it is not unemployment that causes ill health but another third variable which causes ill health and at the same time unemployment. It is known that working class men are more likely to be unemployed at any point in time compared with middle class men. In addition, and probably for independent reasons (see Chapter 7), working class men are likely to have more illnesses and to have higher mortality than middle class men. Therefore in any sample of unemployed men there is likely to be a higher proportion of working class men who in their turn are more likely to be ill. A correlation therefore might be expected between unemployment and ill health, but it is not a causal one.

   This explanation can be examined more closely by controlling for the third variable. This is done by looking at illness patterns within social class groups. If illness is linked to unemployment rather than social class, then holding social class steady by, say, looking at all men in social class V and comparing those who are employed and unemployed, then any differences must be independent of social class. When this is done there is still a 20–30% excess mortality in the unemployed (Moser *et al.*, 1984).

   One study which did examine another variable in the link between unemployment and ill health was an investigation of parasuicide (attempted suicide) in Edinburgh (Platt and Kreitman, 1984). Looking at small areas of the city, they discovered a high correlation between unemployment and parasuicide. After controlling out social class this correlation was reduced but was still significant: in other words there was a still a strong link between the experience of unemployment and attempted suicide. However after controlling for yet another variable, namely poverty, the relationship between unemployment and parasuicide disappeared. This suggests that poverty had a more important role to play in the creation of parasuicide than unemployment, though both poverty and unemployment are clearly linked.

2. It is possible that there is a causal link between unemployment and ill health but that the relationship is the reverse temporal order. In other words, ill health tends to cause unemployment.

All unemployed men do not become ill, it is only a greater tendency to be ill which shows up in the figures. But maybe this observed correlation between unemployment and ill health is caused by the greater likelihood of ill people being made unemployed. In other words if a factory is going to make, say, 10% of its workforce redundant, it is probably more likely to offer redundancy to those workers whose health record is in some way impaired. In effect there would be a selection factor in the creation of unemployment which would tend to push the ill members of the population into the unemployed group.

To test for this explanation it is necessary to look at changes over time. Ideally one would start with a healthy work force and examine their illness and unemployment career thereafter. In practice this is difficult to achieve. One study which attempted it looked at the health records of school leavers and followed them for several years examining their employment record and their further health changes (Banks and Jackson, 1982). It was found that those school leavers who were unemployed did seem to experience more minor psychiatric disease even allowing for their original health status.

Another study to look at this question involved examining the mortality records of men over a 10-year period. They started with a group of men in 1971 who were either in employment or unemployed and seeking work (Moser *et al.*, 1984). Permanently unemployed people who were chronically sick were excluded from the study. The results showed that the group of men seeking work in 1971 had particularly high mortality rates in the following decade from cancers, accidents, poisoning and violence. The other interesting finding in the study was that wives of unemployed men also had relatively high mortality rates, suggesting a direct effect of unemployment rather than a selection effect.

Again it is possible to explain the findings of this study with reference to other variables. The study itself allowed for the effect of social class, to show that the impact of unemployment seemed to be independent of social standing. But it is still possible that those men seeking work in 1971 were in some way less healthy than their working colleagues, and this could explain their increased mortality. Equally it is known that mortality between spouses is linked: the death of one spouse is more likely to be followed by the death of the other. Therefore the higher mortality rates in the wives of unemployed men may also be accounted for by this other intra-family dynamic factor, rather than by unemployment itself.

The studies linking unemployment and ill health demonstrate some of the great difficulties in disentangling causal relationships in the social sciences. As the matter stands, it is probably fair to say that the evidence points to a causal link between unemployment and ill health, but conclusive proof does not exist. It is always possible for a critic to suggest alternative hypotheses for the findings of most studies. Nevertheless because the relationship is both difficult to disentangle, and perhaps inconclusive, it does not mean that it can be ignored.

● **References**

Arber, S. (1987) Social class, non-employment, and chronic illness: continuing the inequalities in health debate. *British Medical Journal,* **294**, 1069–1073

Arber, S., Gilbert, G. N. and Dale, A. (1985) Paid employment and women's health: a benefit or a source of role strain? *Sociology of Health and Illness,* **7**, 375–400

Banks, M. H. and Jackson, P. R. (1982) Unemployment and risk of minor psychiatric disorder in young people: cross-sectional and longitudinal evidence. *Psychological Medicine,* **12**, 789–798

Bentham, G. (1988) Migration and morbidity: implications for geographical studies of disease. *Social Science and Medicine,* **26**, 49–54

Donovan, J. (1984) Ethnicity and health: a research review. *Social Science and Medicine,* **19**, 663–670

Jenkins, R. (1985) Sex differences in minor psychiatric morbidity: a survey of a homogeneous population. *Social Science and Medicine,* **20**, 887–899

Littlewood, R. and Lipsedge, M. (1981) *Aliens and Alienists: Ethnic Minorities and Psychiatry,* Penguin, London

Marmot, M. G. and Syme, S. L. (1976) Acculturation and coronary heart disease in Japanese Americans. *American Journal of Epidemiology,* **104**, 225–247

Marmot, M., Adelskin, A. M. and Bulusu, L. (1984) Immigrant mortality in England and Wales, 1970–78. *OPCS Studies on Medical and Population Subjects,* No. 47, HMSO, London

Moser, K. A., Fox, A. J. and Jones, D. R. (1984) Unemployment and mortality in the OPCS longitudinal study. *Lancet,* **ii**, 1324–1328

Moser, K. A., Goldblatt, P. O., Fox, A. J. *et al.* (1987) Unemployment and mortality: a comparison of the 1971 and 1981 longitudinal study census samples. *British Medical Journal,* **294**, 86–90

Nathanson, C. A. (1977) Sex, illness, and medical care: a review of data, theory and method. *Social Science and Medicine,* **11**, 13–25

Platt, S. and Kreitman, N. (1984) Unemployment and parasuicide in Edinburgh, 1968–82. *British Medical Journal,* **289**, 1029–1032

Waldron, I. (1976) Why do women live longer than men? *Social Science and Medicine,* **10**, 240–262

Wells, N. (1987) *Women's Health Today,* OHE, London

7

Social patterns of illness: II

● Age

As the nineteenth century epidemiologists observed, overall mortality is closely related to age. It is not however a simple linear relationship but rather a lopsided U-curve. This is because mortality is still, despite major improvements since the nineteenth century, relatively high in infants under one year old; mortality then declines rapidly before picking up again in middle age and rising steeply in the elderly. In keeping with this distribution of all deaths, many specific causes of death are similarly closely related with increasing age. For example, cancer and ischaemic heart disease, the major causes of death in the Western world, are much more common in the elderly than in the young. On the other hand, some diseases stand out as being only found in younger age groups: for example, certain leukaemias are mostly found in childhood.

The pattern for mortality and its link with age is therefore clear-cut. There is similar supportive evidence to suggest that morbidity in general is closely linked with age. The elderly report more illnesses; in studies of the prevalence of chronic illness, using activities of daily living as a measure, most of the illness is concentrated among the elderly; and from caseload data it is known that they go more frequently to the doctor.

It is customary to presume that the relationship between chronological age and illness is a product of biological decline associated with the ageing process. However, it is possible to argue that ageing is also a sociocultural process, and some of the health problems of older people relate to the social process of ageing rather than the biological. Support for this argument can be obtained from three sources:

1. The massive improvements in overall life expectancy over the last century or so suggest that many deaths are not as biologically inevitable as once believed. It is now known that one of the prime determinants of infant mortality is not the fixed biological nature of the infant, but rather its environment. Improvements to standard of living, such as have occurred since the nineteenth century, have also reduced infant mortality (McKeown, 1979).

   Similarly many of the diseases of ageing have been shown to have environmental/social causes. It has been calculated that up to 80% of all cancers are environmentally produced. Smoking, diet, exercise, etc. have all been implicated in ischaemic heart disease which is highly correlated with age. All of these factors suggest that the biological decline of the body is not as fixed as it was assumed and it would appear that social factors play a part in the illnesses of ageing as much as biological.

2. There is evidence that many of the so-called biological changes with ageing are in fact culturally specific. In other words, the biological changes known to accompany ageing in our society are not found in other societies. For example, blood pressure is known to increase with age – in some people excessively so, producing hypertension; but in other societies there is no increase with age (Henry and Cassel, 1969). Therefore, it is possible that many of the changes which have so far been accepted as inevitable are in fact the product of environmental conditions in our society.

3. The final piece of evidence which suggests that ageing has a social component as well as a biological one is the specific way our culture treats old people. Several years ago there was a theory that elderly people gradually disengage from social life. In part, this was believed to be due to biological changes which prevented them from participating fully in usual activities, and in part because of their desire to leave the hurry and bustle of everyday life. In retrospect this theory is now seen to be mistaken, and it is possible that many old people were 'disengaged' whether they wanted to or not. As labelling theory suggests (see Chapter 5), treating old people as if they were disengaging is likely to produce the very phenomenon that it predicts. From what we now know of the importance of labelling and social support, it would appear that this forcible disengagement might have had damaging effects on their health. In this way it can be seen that it is not only the biological make-up of old people which determines their illnesses, but also their presumed biological make-up, which then affects the social reaction to and treatment of old people and, in its turn, their illnesses.

● **Social class**

In the nineteenth century it had been observed that certain causes of mortality seemed to be linked to various occupations and occupational groups. In part this was a result of specific work hazards; but occupation was also linked to way of life, which might be related to illness. For example, certain occupations were far better paid than others, meaning that the person concerned could expect better housing, nutrition, etc.

In an attempt to encapsulate these wider aspects of occupations, the British Registrar General early in the twentieth century devised a system of classifying occupation into eight different groups, or social classes, which would convey something of their social standing and skills. The Registrar General then showed a close relationship between each social class and its overall infant mortality rate (deaths of children under the age of one divided by a denominator of the live births during the year). In short, these groupings of occupations were powerfully predictive of the health risk to infants born into these classes; and these risks to infants seemed not directly to be related to the specific work hazards of particular occupations.

The Registrar General later reduced the social classes from eight to five groups. These are given in Table 7.1. Other systems of social stratification exist – the A to E system used to describe consumers in market research, the division

Table 7.1 Social classes

Social class I	Professional	
Social class II	Employers and managers	Middle or non-manual class
Social class III non-manual	Intermediate and junior non-manual	
Social class III manual	Skilled manual and own account non-professional	
Social class IV	Semi-skilled manual and personal services	Working or manual class
Social class V	Unskilled manual	

into a larger number of socioeconomic groups, etc. – but all follow a similar pattern. In a lot of research the different social class groups are aggregated to form two broad divisions which are given different labels: either non-manual, white collar or working class, or manual, blue collar or middle class.

In principle people are assigned to a social class on the basis of their occupation; in practice it is not quite so simple.

First there are many people without an occupation so that it is difficult to classify them. The general rule that has grown up is that the key to this difficulty is the occupation of the male head of household. This means that children can be classified by their father's occupation, as can be wives not in the labour market. However the retired, the unemployed, single women, and working wives still pose difficulties – as well as some occupational groups which do not fall within the classification such as students and the armed forces. Sometimes such people are simply omitted from the analysis; alternatively other ways can be found of classifying them: retired and unemployed can be assigned to the group of their last occupation, single women can be classified according to their own occupation, and working women to their husband's social class.

The assignment of women, even with their own jobs, to their husband's social class has recently come in for severe criticism. Why should women be classified according to their husband's occupation rather than their own in some Victorian display of male supremacy in the family? The arguments against this criticism are:

1. It would still leave non-working women to be classified by their husband's occupation.
2. Most women in the labour force work in social class III jobs so that classifying them according to their own occupations would lose some of the discriminatory power of having them more separated in their husbands' classes.
3. At the end of the day it is the power of social class to explain illness that counts and in some ways it seems that the occupation of the male head of household is a better predictor of illness than the woman's.

Part of the problem is in deciding whether social class is a property of an individual or a household, and this again relates to which has the greater explanatory power. One solution to these difficulties is to change the classification system to make it easier to accommodate these other groups in the population and various attempts are underway to develop a new classification which will still relate to health but will be easier to operate.

These social classes have been shown to have an important relationship to health and illness.

1. Mortality in all age groups is known to vary by social class. Stillbirths, perinatal mortality (stillbirths plus deaths in the first week of life), infant mortality, childhood mortality and adult mortality in all age cohorts is known to be greater in social class V compared with social class I, with a gradient between the two.
2. The more limited evidence that exists for the distribution of morbidity throughout the community (see Chapter 3) would indicate that social class is closely linked to this measure of illness. Thus, for example, surveys which explore self-reported morbidity, both acute and chronic, suggest more illness in social class V compared with social class I with the familiar gradient between the two.
3. Subjective measures of health status suggest worse health for those lower down the social class scale. For example, a social class profile established using the Nottingham Health Profile found that for energy, pain, emotional reactions, sleep and physical mobility there was a clear class gradient with those lower on the social class scale having the worst health. There was no clear class pattern with the sixth dimension, namely social isolation (Hunt et al., 1986).

Social class differences in health have been of particular interest to sociologists for two reasons:

1. The notion of social class has a wider significance in sociology, which makes it of particular interest in the explanation of health differences. Many sociologists believe that the social class divisions of modern Western societies are fundamental to understanding how the latter change and maintain stability. The links with health are therefore just one more facet of a much larger explanatory model.
2. Related to the above, social class is correlated with many other features of modern society. Social class correlates with income, housing, education, leisure activities, diet, etc. so that each of these is also likely to be linked with illness.

Explaining social class and health

Various possible explanations have been advanced for the observed close association between health and social class.

Material explanations
One of the remarkable features of social class stratification is how it relates to many other aspects of life such as income, education, housing, etc. This means that working class people have poorer access to resources than middle class, and this has led to a claim that this relative material deprivation is the major factor in producing higher morbidity and mortality in working class groups.

This explanation certainly has appeal. It was in fact the major explanation accepted by the Black Report, a working party set up to look at social class inequalities in the context of the NHS (Townsend and Davidson, 1982). Because the relationship between social class, health and material resources is so close and consistent, it does provide a very strong case that these material circumstances are implicated in the causation of illness. Furthermore, the evidence from the nineteenth century, discussed in Chapter 6, supports the idea that it is relative standard of living which is the major determinant of health status. If this is correct then material deprivation could be corrected by directing additional resources towards those families in need (Townsend *et al.*, 1988).

Nevertheless, while the association between social class and illness is very close, and the general argument apparently so reasonable, critics can point to the lack of specific explanations linking material deprivation to ill health.

Diet, and other behaviours which might be influenced by poor resources, have been suggested as of aetiological significance. But the relationship between specific dietary habits and disease is not at all clear-cut. Dietary items such as cholesterol and fibre may be important but their exact role in the causation of many diseases remains confused. The very fact that there is such debate about the effects of these specific dietary factors also suggests that their effects, if shown, will not be large enough to explain the size of social class variation.

In the nineteenth century the link between the poor housing of the working class and illness was probably mainly brought about by lack of running water and unhygienic conditions. Today it is more likely to be relative overcrowding, dampness and coldness in winter, but it is difficult to correlate high overall mortality with each of these factors. Specific cases can be pointed to, such as hypothermia amongst old people, or asthma and chest infections in children, but on their own these are insufficient to explain the very large differences in morbidity and mortality between the social classes.

Nevertheless, housing may be important because in recent years it has been suggested that housing tenure may give a better prediction of the distribution of illness in a community than social class itself. It has been found, for example, that owner occupiers are more likely to have better health, at least as measured by mortality, than those in rented accommodation. Housing tenure, of course, cuts across social class: middle class people tend to be owner occupiers, but there are people with social class I jobs who live in rented accommodation and equally people with social class V jobs who own their own house. But in these instances the type of housing tenure seems more important than social class in predicting health status. This may have something to do with the quality of the housing, but equally housing tenure may also reflect other attributes of the person such as income, job security, independence, etc. which in their turn may be the real determinants of health.

In summary, there are some specific diseases which can be precisely related to working class material deprivation. For example, accidents in childhood, both in the home and outside, probably relate to poor domestic facilities and lack of safe playing areas outside the home. But taken together all of these various known specific links between material circumstance and illness do not add up to an adequate explanation for the large differences between social classes.

A much more powerful explanation of illness is afforded by specific habits such as cigarette smoking. At first sight smoking is not a measure of deprivation but of relative prosperity given that the habit is so expensive. Nevertheless, it has been argued that smoking is in fact a response to material deprivation. A working class family, without the material resources which may be commonplace for a middle class family, may find that smoking is a means of coping with their lives (Graham, 1987). In this sense, smoking is a consequence of material deprivation and the high morbidity and mortality which can be associated with it supports the notion that it is material deprivation which produces illness. Alternatively the smoking evidence can be used to argue that it is not material deprivation but beliefs and customs of the social class group which produces illness.

Cultural explanations

It is known that different societies, even at the same stage of economic development, have different patterns of disease. For example, the major cause of death amongst men in the United States is ischaemic heart disease, whilst in Japan it is strokes (cerebrovascular accidents). However when Japanese men emigrate to the United States and become acculturated to that society then their mortality pattern changes as they come to die more frequently from ischaemic heart disease (Marmot et al., 1975). This phenomenon cannot be explained in terms of material deprivation, as the standard of living between Japan and the USA are similar. The only alternative is that it is something to do with Japanese way of life and, conversely, US way of life, that contributes to the particular disease patterns found in those societies. It may be nutrition, other behaviours, or family dynamics, but whatever it is, it is rooted in the particular cultural milieu in which people find themselves.

This argument can be applied to social class differences in health. In many ways middle and working class groups constitute different cultures. They have different habits, read different newspapers, watch different television programmes, have different leisure activities, have different outlooks on life, and so on. This can be seen, for example, in poor working class support for disease prevention programmes.

Even if some class differences in health can be explained by different class cultures, there is probably still a close relationship with material deprivation. The culture itself may be a response to long-term material deprivation, and the culture may, in various ways, hinder material improvement. One theory in the 1960s was that as living standards for working class people improved then they would start to endorse a middle class way of life. A major study of the relatively affluent workers in a car plant showed that despite their increased income, working class culture still prevailed: there may be change, but it is likely to be long-term.

If the material explanation is correct then there is a direct policy implication: material deprivation can be corrected by allocating corrective resources. However, if a cultural explanation is correct, then the policy implications are more difficult. First, it is probably that much more difficult to change a cultural pattern. Campaigns, for example, to get working class people to stop smoking have been largely unsuccessful. Secondly, there is an ethical issue in trying to change aspects of culture. If, for example, a working class man smokes because he finds pleasure in the activity, and he is less concerned about the long-term consequences, do middle class health professionals have a right to tell him that his values are mistaken, and that he should substitute deferred gratification for immediate? There is evidence that cigarette smoking is an integral component of the lifestyle of many working class people; is it morally right to try and change this for a middle class value?

Artefact explanations

The central feature of the artefact explanation is that the observed and supposedly causal relationship between social class and illness is spurious: it is not that social class causes illness, but that in some way illness causes the person to belong to a particular social class (Bloor *et al.*, 1987). Three variants of this position can be identified:

Drift and social class. Social class links with illness are determined by identifying a person's occupation, which places them in a social class, and correlating this class position with their health status. But perhaps it is not occupation/social class which influences illness but illness which influences social class. For example, a social class I lawyer with schizophrenia may be unable to continue in his or her chosen occupation and eventually take a relatively unskilled job. This phenomenon may therefore account for at least some of the excess numbers of social class V people with schizophrenia.

The argument might also apply to other diseases, such as heart and respiratory diseases, which might cause someone to change their occupation. Thus, it is possible that the social class variation in illness is a product of occupational changes following the advent of illness, rather than the other way round.

There is now fairly good evidence that for certain diseases occupational 'drift' is a component of the explanation of social class variation. However, for some diseases it may be more likely that manual workers have to turn to non-manual work. In other words there may be some drift towards social class III clerical jobs and away from social class IV and V manual jobs. Also, given that the major causes of death are ischaemic heart disease, cancer and stroke, it is difficult to identify how these would better enable middle class people to carry out working class jobs. And the same goes for chronic illness which in many ways is more likely to be manageable in middle class occupations compared with working.

Infant mortality and social class. Is it possible that the observed relationship between social class and illness is simply a product of the way that social class itself is measured? This hypothesis arose out of the way that social class was originally derived by the Registrar General at the beginning of the century. A description of what he did will illustrate the argument.

The Registrar General described a relationship between social class and infant mortality, such that the professional classes had a much lower rate than manual occupations. He showed this by assigning all occupations to eight different categories, and then showing that the categories, in their turn, related to infant mortality. But how did he assign occupations to these eight different categories?

The assignment could not have been an entirely arbitrary procedure otherwise he would have found no relationship with infant mortality. It is therefore possible that he already knew the infant mortality rate of each occupational group, and used this as the basis of assignment; in other words, he might have assigned occupations with a high infant mortality rate to a low social class and vice versa. His finding that social class was related to infant mortality would therefore be an artefact of his measuring process: yes, there was a relationship between the two, but only because social class had been defined in terms of infant mortality (Jones and Cameron, 1984).

No-one would suggest that the Registrar General deliberately 'fixed' his findings, but nor is anyone sure of what he actually did do. He may, as he suggested himself, have assigned occupations on the basis of social standing, which would have embraced those crucial aspects of social class such as housing, behaviour, education, wealth, etc. which were then, as now, believed to have a powerful influence on infant mortality. The suspicion however remains that there is something slightly circular about the method of constructing his occupational groupings.

The suspicion of some circularity in the relationship between social class and health is reinforced by the knowledge that occupations are regularly reassigned between social classes. Thus, every ten years the distribution of occupations in their social classes is reassessed, and sometimes occupations are moved. This is justified on the grounds that the work of specific occupations can change with supply and demand in the economy, new technology, and the acquisition of new skills. On these grounds, an occupation which might have been decidedly unskilled 50 years ago would now be seen as skilled and vice versa. It is therefore important that this change is recognized in the social class classification. But what is it about an occupation that changes to sufficient extent to justify reassignment? No doubt it is the whole panoply of social class indicators such as income, education, housing, etc. which helps determine this; but also, perhaps, it is the occupation's infant mortality rate and/or health status (which correlates with these other attributes of social class) which affects assignment, even if indirectly. In this way the continuing social class differential in mortality this century could be an artefact of constant reclassifications: whenever an occupation improves its mortality rate it is simply moved up the scale to a new class, so to leave the old class with a residuum of high risk occupations.

While this explanation may have appeal for conspiracy theorists, social class membership is not simply determined by health status. As pointed out above, social class also correlates highly with many other facets of living. In this way it appears a more meaningful category than if it had been arbitrarily determined. Nevertheless, it is still possible that a certain amount of the observed gradient between social classes has been maintained by the regular reassignment of some occupations. This means that mortality data by social class from one decade are not directly comparable with mortality data by social class from another; some studies have tried to correct for this reassignment factor, but they cannot correct for the fact that the mix of occupations in a social class changes as does the nature of occupations themselves.

If assignment of occupations was based on health status then some degree of homogeneity might be expected between the social classes. However, what is remarkable is the great diversity of health status even within a social class. In other words, the construction of social classes may be concealing differences rather than amplifying them. This view is supported by a study of different grades of civil servants which showed the gradient between high and low to be considerably greater than their nominal class position would indicate (Rose and Marmot, 1981).

Social class and ischaemic heart disease. The final artefactual explanation relates not to overall mortality and morbidity rates but to specific causes. It is now known that social classes IV and V have a higher mortality from ischaemic heart disease than social classes I and II. Twenty years ago, however, the relationship was the other way round. It is now suggested that the inverse relationship in the past was an artefact of the measuring process. This could have come about for two reasons:

1. Cause of death is established by clinicians and pathologists. There are, no doubt, fashions in diagnosis and it is possible that in the inter-war years the relatively newly fashionable label of coronary heart disease was diagnosed more frequently in middle class people than in working class.

    In the inter-war years many people received a diagnosis of myocardial degeneration; this diagnosis is now not acceptable, and in retrospect many of these deaths may well have been cases of ischaemic heart disease. In other words it is possible that if diagnostic fashions are class-related, then this may produce artificial excesses or shortages of particular illnesses in different social groups.

2. The other reason for a falsely high rate of deaths from ischaemic heart disease in middle class men relates to the numerators and denominators used in the calculation. To determine a rate of ischaemic heart disease deaths, the number of deaths from the disease in a particular group must be known as well as the numbers at risk. Thus, the social class death rate for ischaemic heart disease involves dividing the numerator of number of deaths in a particular class by the denominator which would be the total numbers in that social class in the population. (These respective figures would usually also be age and sex standardized to allow for age and sex variations between social classes.)

    The denominator is determined from census data which are produced every ten years. The census asks a question about occupation which enables numbers in each social class (and therefore 'at risk') to be determined. The numerator is obtained from death certificates which record from the relatives the deceased's last occupation. Thus error can creep in from using a denominator which is out of date or a numerator which is inaccurate.

    The existence of an apparent excess number of deaths from ischaemic heart disease among middle class men led to the 1960's belief in diseases of affluence: that the ravages of disease which had so afflicted the poor in the nineteenth century were now turning their attention to the rich. In retrospect this argument is now seen to be mistaken because it is unlikely that middle class people at the period did have excessive mortality from ischaemic heart disease. Moreover, it is also mistaken to argue that our society is characterized by diseases of affluence. Certainly there are diseases brought about by over-consumption, alcoholism being one, but by and large the illnesses in our community seem to be linked, as in the nineteenth century, with deprivation in its widest sense.

●   **References**

Bloor, M., Samphier, M. and Prior, L. (1987) Artefact explanations of inequalities in health: an assessment of the evidence. *Sociology of Health and Illness*, **9**, 231–264

Graham, H. (1987) Women's smoking and family health. *Social Science and Health*, **25**, 47–56

Henry, J. P. and Cassel, J. C. (1969) Psychosocial factors in essential hypertension. *American Journal of Epidemiology,* **90**, 171–200

Hunt, S., McEwen, J. and McKenna, S. P. (1986) *Measuring Health Status,* Croom Helm, London

Jones, I. G. and Cameron, D. (1984) Social class analysis: an embarrassment to epidemiology. *Community Medicine,* **6**, 37–46

Marmot, M. G. *et al.* (1975) Epidemiological studies of coronary heart disease and stroke in Japanese men living in Japan, Hawaii and California. *American Journal of Epidemiology,* **102**, 514–525

McKeown, T. (1979) *The Role of Medicine,* Blackwell, Oxford

Rose, G. and Marmot, M. (1981) Social class and CHD. *British Heart Journal,* **45**, 13–19

Townsend, P. and Davidson, N. (1982) *The Black Report,* Penguin, London

Townsend, P., Davidson, N. and Whitehead, M. (1988) *Inequalities in Health,* Penguin, London

8

Coping with illness

People cope with illness in a variety of different ways and in so doing call upon a range of resources. Acute illness tends to be the least difficult to manage simply because it is by definition a temporary situation. Chronic illness, on the other hand, tends to require more fundamental readjustments on behalf of both the patient and of the immediate carers. These various coping strategies can, in their turn, help ameliorate the impact of the illness or, in certain circumstances, worsen the situation.

● Managing labels

One response to a diagnostic label is behaviour change (secondary deviance); this consequence of labelling has been discussed in Chapter 5 as part of the social aetiology of illness. But, of course, the reaction which causes illness is also part of the patient's strategy of coping with the illness and its meaning. Particular examples of these strategies can be found in the response to stigma and being institutionalized.

Managing stigma

Goffman suggested that a person with a stigmatizing condition could pursue several strategies which were largely based on the salience of the stigma they carried (Goffman, 1963). On the one hand the stigma could be very obvious to others and therefore be a *discrediting* attribute or, on the other hand, it might be relatively hidden and therefore *discreditable*. A patient with a discrediting attribute has only a limited range of options because the stigma is present for all to see. A patient with a discreditable attribute, however, does have the option of trying to keep the stigma concealed.

1. *Passing*: a person with a discreditable stigma can try and pass as 'normal'. Depending on the medical problem this will often require various forms of subterfuge, with the constant risk of exposure. This latter threat of disclosure and possible shame can be a constant source of psychological tension, so much so that for some it is easier to be open about the stigma.
2. *Covering*: a person with a discrediting attribute has no opportunity to pass, but can still try and minimize the significance of the stigma. This may be by

avoiding situations in which their stigma would be made salient, or by reducing the visibility of the problem that is stigmatized.

3. *Withdrawal*: the avoidance of difficult social situations can be taken further by deliberately withdrawing from social life. In this way the stigmatized avoid all contacts which might produce embarrassment or shame.

In Goffman's analysis all stigmatized people wish to hide away their shameful marks; moreover he presents a stigmatized attribute as something a person has or does not have. However, more recent studies described below suggest that the picture is not so clear: some people, for example, deliberately 'come out' with their disabilities, while others are never sure from one day to the next whether they have a stigmatizing attribute or not. Even so the coping strategies that Goffman outlines are a useful way of understanding some of the ways in which people manage labels.

Institutionalization

A particular variant of secondary deviance of importance to medicine is the process known as 'institutionalization' (Jones and Fowles, 1984). It is now well established that if a person is placed in an institution such as a prison or a mental hospital for many years then their attitudes and behaviour change. It is clear that in an institution with its own set of rules and routines, inmate behaviour, however resistant at first, will gradually change towards conformity, if only to make the daily routine more manageable (Goffman, 1961).

This process of conformity is often considerably aided by the practices of many institutions which have the effect of 'depersonalizing' the inmate on first admission. Personal effects are rarely allowed and private space or activities are kept to a minimum. The effect is to reinforce the exclusion of the inmate's 'old' self and the emergence of a new institutionalized identity. Inmates must adjust to new routines of sleeping, eating, relaxing, defaecating, etc. which have often been introduced for the benefit of the staff and institution rather than for the needs of the patient. (Because of the difficulties for staff in identifying short-term goals in chronic care, many seem to resort to 'goal displacement' in which the rather general and woolly end-point of 'care' gets displaced in favour of specific short-term targets such as finishing meals by a certain time or ensuring that the laundry is efficiently managed.)

The problem with this new identity and patient readjustment is that though it might be suitable for living within an institution it is inappropriate for life outside. In particular the dependency which institutions create in their inmates means that they have great difficulty in adapting to independence outside its walls. Dependence is, of course, exacerbated by the fact that most of those hospitalized for a long period are precisely those who through mental or physical impairment are unable to cope on their own.

These effects are well known and there is now a policy to try to prevent institutionalization by keeping people in the community for long-term treatment – though the effectiveness and rationale for this has been challenged (Scull, 1977). Otherwise some of the effects of institutions can be minimized by shortening the length of each stay and by trying to reduce some of the more stark, depersonalizing features of an institutional atmosphere. Furthermore, even when treatment does require lengthy hospitalization specific attention can be directed towards maintaining or re-establishing the patient's autonomy through some form of mental or physical 'rehabilitation'.

• Coping with chronic illness

The labelling perspective laid the foundations for a fundamentally social view of disability by arguing that the doctor's answer to the medical question 'What is it (the disease)?' could also become the patient's answer to their question 'Who am I?'. Thus a medical diagnosis, accurate and made in good faith, could become the new 'master' identity for the patient. Such new identities were deviant ones, so patients had to contend with a role of social outcast.

While helping to explain the effects of illness on the patient, the labelling perspective can in some ways be a too mechanistic, almost behaviourist, model in which labels produce their effects with minimal involvement of the patient; indeed it seems less the label itself which is of importance than the reaction (which might even be to an 'imagined' label). In addition labelling can seem a limited explanation: certainly people respond to stimuli/labels but why do certain labels have this effect and not others, and why do some people produce a greater reaction than others? The sociological answer has been an increasing emphasis on patients' meanings, and with it new methods of investigation.

Very broadly there are two ways of approaching the study of human behaviour. The first, taking its cue from the natural sciences, is to seek explanation in terms of causes. Thus, were labels held to 'cause' a response in the patient, a study might somehow measure labelling and the response, and correlate the two. If the temporal order was correct and there were no extraneous variables to contaminate the correlation, the result would confirm the hypothesis. This model lays human behaviour open to the same sorts of explanation that characterize medical diseases themselves. The difficulty is that human behaviour is not the same type of phenomenon as, say, inflammation. Not least, inflammation remains much the same whatever the measurement procedure, whereas a question to a patient on, say, their emotional well-being or the state of their marriage has already contaminated the result.

There are techniques available which attempt to minimize the methodological biases associated with researching a 'knowing subject', but there is in addition an even more fundamental conceptual difficulty, namely the role of reasons and meaning in social life. Inflammation responds to stimuli which are somehow external to it, whereas people respond to meanings which are inherently internal. Thus while poor interpersonal relationships, anxiety or immobility may be seen as 'causes' of experiencing increased pain, the critic can argue this is just a shorthand: what actually happens is that the patient interprets these events and it is the meanings given them which are inseparable from the actual experience. Thus all symptoms are percepts and intimately related to the human being as an interpreting animal.

This form of argument has led to the development of methods to investigate meanings. These methods tend to be ethnographic, treating each person as a stranger. The approach produces intensive descriptive studies of small groups of people, in each case trying to establish how the person makes sense of the world. Society is not 'out there' but inside people; the social reaction can only therefore be studied by exploring this internalized social world: 'What do people make of the reaction of others?', 'How do they manage?', 'What does it mean to them?', 'How do they go about answering the question: "Who am I?"?'.

Patient meanings

The labelling approach argues that in giving a diagnosis, medicine gives a master label to the patient, especially the disabled. This simple view has been challenged by the claim that patient self-definition is an altogether more complex procedure than this (Safilios-Rothschild, 1970). In interviews with a group of disabled people it was found that disability seemed to have different meanings and different consequences from more traditional 'illness' or 'disease', yet these self-definitions were by and large ignored by the health professionals who had *their* view of what the disabled role should be and used their influence to persuade the disabled to accept it. Indeed the disabled were like any minority group, in Safilios-Rothschild's view, who had their 'real' wishes and potential defined by others. Health professionals, she argued, make judgements on behalf of the disabled without asking the individuals about their problems, preferred solutions, and alternatives or by openly disregarding all information received from the disabled persons themselves about desirable goals and solutions (Safilios-Rothschild, 1976).

The complexities surrounding the development of disabled peoples' self-perception was further explored by Blaxter (1976) in a study of 194 physically impaired patients. She found that the whole question of who was disabled could not be answered as neatly as had been assumed because the boundary between disabled and non-disabled seemed constantly blurred both at the 'official' level, and more importantly at the level of self-definition. The health and welfare services did not produce a massive and overwhelming 'labelling' effect since they themselves were confused about who was to count as 'disabled'. In part this was because of important differences in the way different sectors of the welfare state classified disability, but also because of uncertainty on the part of individual professionals as to whether a label of disability at a particular time would help or harm the patient. Added to this the so-called disabled themselves showed marked temporal variation in their own assessments of whether they really were disabled and/or its severity.

Blaxter therefore argued that the disabled were not a homogeneous group and the 'label' to be affixed to someone was the result of negotiation between patient and professional. Patients could reject a label just as much as they could accept one; indeed the identity of 'disabled' might change considerably over time. The important feature of this process, Blaxter suggested, was the patient's own 'constructions', which might be quite at variance with medical views; indeed she found that the patients' attempts to make sense of their illness often produced accounts markedly different from those in their medical records, and this could create problems in terms of adjustment and rehabilitation.

Goffman's analysis suggested that disability was an unambiguous status, but for many diseases this assumption seems unwarranted in view of the ambivalent and changeable response of patients to the question of who they are. The very fact that the course of the disease and self-definition are uncertain on even a day-to-day basis means that the strategies themselves have to be similarly varied, covering up one moment to avoid stigma or the threat of dependency, and eliciting help the next. The uncertainty about the course of the disease allows the patient at one time to hope for relief or remission, while at another dreading a deterioration or relapse. In effect, as Wiener (1975) observed in a study of rheumatoid arthritics, such patients were engaged in a continuous and precarious balancing of options. Every day was a mental trial: people did not 'adjust' or 'come to terms' with their disability as health care professionals might imagine; rather they tried constantly to devise a viable strategy for getting through each and every day, constantly varying their self-definitions to cope with the immediate problems of living.

Cognitions and health

The self-definition of need is intimately related to the self-definition of disability. Health and social welfare agencies traditionally have tended to define what disabled people 'need' in terms of services. But their notions might be far removed from that of the patient and Blaxter, in her study of physically impaired patients, identified several types of problem which seemed related to activities of everyday living: job problems to do with finding, maintaining and adjusting to work; money problems; and social problems associated with establishing and maintaining relationships (1976). Blaxter's analysis of the interviews enabled her to identify three-quarters of the sample as having at least one problem in one of her predefined areas in the survey year; of these, less than half were solved during the year. Thus she claimed that there were real patient-defined needs going unmet in her population.

Blaxter's list of unmet needs was added to by a not dissimilar study by Locker (1983). Locker interviewed a sample of diagnosed rheumatoid arthritics. Like Blaxter, he was concerned with patients' self-definitions of their problems, but the 'problem areas' he identified were different in various ways. Following Blaxter, he found that occupational and relationship problems were important, as were practical difficulties of everyday living. In addition he identified the medical problems specifically arising from the disease, such as managing the drug regimen. But in addition he identified patients' cognitive problems in attempting to make sense of the onset, course and future of the disorder and also problems in understanding the workings of the medical and welfare agencies which offer treatment and social support.

The idea that patients' cognitions were important was relatively new. The traditional medical model would presumably claim that a patient's knowledge of his or her illness came from directly experiencing it and this knowledge, conceptualized as reports of symptoms, was a useful component of the medical history. Thereafter the patient did not need knowledge other than to report symptom changes, as diagnosis and treatment could occur independently of the patient's own perceptions of the nature of the illness.

Such a model of doctor–patient communication, however, does not seem so applicable to chronic and disabling illnesses in which 'recovery' is not the norm: part of medical management requires the provision of an explanation. But it was not simply a case of telling everything, in that doctors resort to what Blaxter referred to as 'information management'. Because of the frequent clinical uncertainty of both diagnosis and prognosis, doctors feel constrained to control the amount of explanation given to the patient at any point in time. But equally, certain information is withheld from the patient as part of the overall case management. In effect, information transfer has become one of the therapeutic tools in an often limited range.

Locker's study, however, picked up on an important current of thought that extended the significance of patient knowledge. The patients' knowledge was no longer perceived as being restricted to the experience of symptoms, and the doctor's role that of providing explanation. The terms 'lay theories' or 'explanatory models' were coined to describe this knowledge because it seemed, in its own terms, as coherent and sophisticated as medical theories (see Chapter 2). True, medicine might view some aspect of the patient's theory as 'mistaken', but are the criteria medicine used to identify truth and error the same as or wholly relevant to patients? Moreover, at a practical level, changing one element in a patient's cohesive theory by 'educating the patient' looks remarkably difficult to achieve.

Patient theories or cognitions are also important in their implications for an effective and harmonious doctor–patient interaction. As Locker claimed, cognitions become one of the resources which the chronically sick and disabled command. In effect, physical impairment and social handicap are not simply linked through the reactions of others (see Chapter 5) but also through the patient's own cognitions. Thus it is possible to distinguish 'experienced' from 'felt' stigma in that it is not the social reaction which produces social disability but the disabled's own self-perceptions of those reactions (Scambler, 1984).

In the light of these cognitive models the issue of disability and self-identity can be readdressed. In Bury's (1982) study of another group of rheumatoid arthritics, he again noted the day-to-day struggle to cope with the disease, characterizing its principal effects on a wider canvas as 'biographical disruption'. Bury argued that the 'taken-for-granted' assumptions and commonsense boundaries, which everyone establishes to make life manageable, are breached by some patients. Not only has everyday life to be renegotiated but the disruption to 'explanatory systems' used by everyone requires a fundamental re-thinking of the person's own biography and self-concepts, which in turn throws into relief the cognitive and material resources available to the individual.

Contrary to the usual criticism of the biomedical model as ignoring the patient, Bury suggested that the otherwise limited medical explanation was an important cognitive resource for the patient. The very fact that doctors, by and large, failed to move away from the 'it' of disease meant that disease was held separate from self. This enabled disease to be maintained at a distance, so that the patient could claim that they were the victims of external forces: patients could therefore answer the question 'Why me?' without the additional burden of responsibility or guilt. True, medical explanation and understanding were both ambiguous and limited, but it still provided at least one relatively fixed point on a terrain of uncertainty.

Experts' meaning systems

Blaming doctors for giving diagnostic labels has largely disappeared, not least because a stark choice between a rehabilitation model, which suggests that doctors should intervene, and a societal reaction model, which suggests that doctors should not intervene, is too simplistic (Gove, 1976). The rehabilitation model would seem preferable but the societal reaction model, which emphasizes the importance of labels, cannot be discarded. Indeed the adoption by the World Health Organization of a classification which separates impairment, disability and handicap is recognition that social reaction has very real effects on patient identity and self-definition (Wood, 1975). The skill is to steer a difficult course between providing help and support, and creating dependency and devalued status.

Medical explanation can form a valued component of how the disabled make sense of their lives, but it would be a mistake to imagine that this is an injunction to 'tell all' to the patient. If recent work in sociology has shown anything, it is the complexity and sophistication of patients' explanatory models and meaning systems. These seem to lie at the heart of how patients cope with their illness on a day-to-day basis. As has been argued in a different setting (Tuckett *et al.*, 1985), there is a case for doctors to recognize their consultations as situations in which explanatory models are exchanged. In this light, use of listening and counselling techniques to elicit their patients' cognitions may further help their patients to live on a day-to-day basis with their illnesses.

● Carers

Illness, as the previous section describes, has fundamental effects on the patients. Not only is their biological functioning impaired in some way, but their psychological and social worlds are disrupted and constantly need managing. In this way it is clear that illness is as much a psychosocial phenomenon as a biological one.

In some ways illness can be seen like ripples on a pond: the biological lesion causes upset to the patient's psychosocial adjustment, but then it moves further out to touch people close to the patient, particularly their immediate carers. Many patients with chronic and debilitating illnesses are very dependent on others for physical and psychological support and the significant role of these carers in helping the ill cope is now well recognized. What is less well understood is the impact of the patient's illness – both its biological nature and its psychosocial reaction – on the health of carers. What little evidence that does exist would suggest major problems with the health of carers as they struggle themselves to cope with an illness that is located in another's body (Lewis and Meredith, 1988).

● References

Blaxter, M. (1976) *The Meaning of Disability,* Heinemann, London

Bury, M. (1982) Chronic illness as biographical disruption. *Sociology of Health and Illness,* **4,** 167–182

Goffman, E. (1961) *Asylums: Essays on the Social Situation of Mental Patients and Other Inmates,* Penguin, London

Goffman, E. (1963) *Stigma: Notes on the Management of Spoiled Identity,* Penguin, London

Gove, W. R. (1976) Societal reaction theory and disability. In *The Sociology of Physical Disability and Rehabilitation* (ed. G. L. Albrecht), University of Pittsburgh Press, Pittsburgh

Jones, K. and Fowles, A. J. (1984) *Ideas on Institutions: Analysing the Literature on Long-term Care and Custody,* Routledge and Kegan Paul, London

Lewis, J. and Meredith, B. (1988) Daughters caring for mothers: the experience of caring and its implications for professional helpers. *Ageing and Society,* **8,** 1–21

Locker, D. (1983) *Disadvantage and Disability,* Tavistock, London

Safilios-Rothschild, C. (1970) *The Sociology and Social Psychology of Disability and Rehabilitation,* Random House, New York

Safilios-Rothschild, C. (1976) Disabled persons' self-definitions and their implications for rehabilitation. In *The Sociology of Physical Disability and Rehabilitation* (ed. G. L. Albrecht), University of Pittsburgh Press, Pittsburgh

Scambler, G. (1984) Perceiving and coping with stigmatizing illness. In *The Experience of Illness* (eds R. Fitzpatrick *et al.*), Tavistock, London, pp. 203–226

Scull, A. T. (1977) *Decarceration,* Prentice Hall, Englewood Cliffs

Tuckett, D., Boulton, M., Olson, C. *et al.* (1985) *Meetings Between Experts: An Approach to Sharing Ideas in Medical Consultations,* Tavistock, London

Wiener, C. (1975) The burden of rheumatoid arthritis: tolerating the uncertainty. *Social Science and Medicine,* **9**, 97–104

Wood, P. (1975) *Classification of Impairments and Handicap,* World Health Organization, Geneva

9

Models of illness

The preceding chapters in this book have illustrated the extent to which the biomedical model is a limited interpretation of the nature of illness. This chapter consolidates this perspective by an examination of the explanatory power of the biomedical model and some alternatives.

● Exploring abdominal pain

The traditional differential diagnosis

Abdominal pain is supposed to arise from the discharge of afferent nerve fibres in and around the abdomen. The pathological basis of the pain includes processes such as inflammation and ischaemia. The history of the pain together with abdominal examination usually lead to a diagnosis: the acute pain of appendicitis is caused by inflammation of the appendix; chronic pain is usually more associated with ulcers or diverticulitis, though there are many other abdominal diseases in the differential diagnosis such as cholecystitis, Crohn's disease, ulcerative colitis, etc.

Abdominal pain in children

Various studies have looked at the incidence and diagnoses of abdominal pain in children. Such pain is fairly common yet it is unusual to find an organic pathological basis for it.

One study which examined this phenomenon in general practice involved collecting all the cases of abdominal pain presenting in children over a seven-year period (Turner, 1978). The sample eventually amounted to 162 children who were investigated as appropriate. Five were found to have a possible organic basis for their pain, which meant that the other 157 had pain of unexplained origin. Medicine often groups these pains together and gives them the label of functional or idiopathic pains, precisely because their origin is unknown.

The study however tried to explore the wider ramifications of the pain by comparing the close relatives of the children with abdominal pain with a control group. It was found that the close relatives of children with abdominal pain:

(i)   consulted more frequently;
(ii) had more abdominal pain and abdominal operations;
(iii) had higher rates of psychiatric illness and referral;
(iv) had more known marital problems.

These findings suggest various hypotheses about the basis of the pain.

1. Many children in the community have abdominal pain, but the amount that is taken to the doctor will very much depend on parental response to the symptoms. If parents are high consulters then by and large they have a higher likelihood of bringing their children's abdominal pain to the doctor. This may well help to explain the higher consultation rates of the parents and relatives of children with abdominal pain.

2. The fact that the parents and relatives themselves have more abdominal pain might suggest two explanations for the child's pain. First, the child observes the abdominal symptoms in the parents and for various reasons mimics them. Alternatively, the parents having experienced abdominal pains may now be more alert to their existence in their children.

3. The higher rates of psychiatric illness and referral observed in the close relatives of children presenting with abdominal pain compared with the control group might suggest either that the child is responding with 'belly aches' to a parent's psychiatric problems, or that the presentation of the child is itself a symptom of the psychiatric illness in the parent. In other words the real patient is not the child but the parent or relative.

4. Similar explanations might apply to the observation that more known marital problems were presented in the close relatives of children with abdominal pain. Either the child in some way is responding to the marital difficulties with pain, or the parents are using the child's illness as a way of showing their own problems: perhaps the child can provide a ticket of entry to the doctor.

In each of these possible explanations the basis of the illness moves from its apparent location in the child's abdomen to the relationships within the family. This supports other well-known evidence that family dynamics are bound up with illness (Meyer and Haggerty, 1962).

Life events and appendicitis

One hundred and nineteen patients between the ages of 13 and 17 presenting with appendicitis and undergoing appendicectomy were identified, together with a similar number of controls (Creed, 1981). The patients and controls were interviewed about life events in the previous year: the total number of events was noted, as was the number classified as 'threatening' and 'severe'.

After these interviews had been completed the pathological reports on the state of the appendix were read. Sixty-three of the appendices (about half) were inflamed and the others were normal. But when this pathological appearance of the appendix was linked to the life events experienced by the patient an interesting picture emerged. Patients experiencing a severe life event in the preceding year were much more likely to have a non-inflamed appendix compared with the rest. In fact the proportion of patients with normal appendices having severe events was remarkably similar to the percentage of patients who were found, in a different study (Brown and Harris, 1978), to be depressed after having severe life events. In addition, compared with a control group, even those patients with a pathologically inflamed appendix showed a much higher rate of threatening life events.

Surgeons are not able to predict the pathological appearance of the appendix: they simply operate when they diagnose a likely inflamed appendix. It is well established, however, that about half of all appendices taken out are pathologically normal, despite the patient having shown all the clinical signs and symptoms of appendicitis. So why do patients get appendicitis, real or apparent? In this study the microscopic appearance of the appendix was somehow linked to the life experiences of the patients in the preceding year. Having a severe life event seemed to be related to having an apparent appendicitis in the same way that it was linked to the onset of depression. In fact when the patients' psychiatric state was assessed, depression rates amongst the non-inflamed appendix patients were twice the rate amongst controls and the inflamed. In other words, it seemed that a severe life event may bring about depression, appendicitis or both.

The pain of appendicitis would appear to have emerged as much from negative life experiences as from the nerve fibres of the abdomen.

Life events and gastrointestinal disorder   *Craig & Brown 84*

A study of life events and gastrointestinal disorder investigated the relationship between patients with abdominal pain referred by general practitioners to gastrointestinal clinics and preceding life events (Craig and Brown, 1984). The proportion of patients reporting life events was then examined in those patients who were shown to have an 'organic' basis for their pain, those without ('functional' pain) and in the controls. Numbers experiencing a severe life event in the preceding 38 weeks were 23%, 57% and 15% respectively. In other words severe events seemed, as in the previous study, to be linked with abdominal pain of unexplained origin. However, like the previous study there also seemed to be a link between severe events and actual pathological lesions inside the abdomen.

Again the pain was located in the abdomen, but the illness, it seemed, was to be found elsewhere.

The traditional model of medicine explains symptoms by trying to identify their origins in a pathological lesion inside the body. The doctor does this by identifying signs, carrying out relevant investigations and making a diagnosis. However, each of the above three studies shows that in many cases the exact nature of the illness could not be diagnosed by simply examining the insides of the body. Each of these three studies could equally imply that the disease existed not under the skin but in the patient's environment, psychological state, coping strategies, social relationships, etc.. This would seem to indicate that medicine should be attending to a wider psychosocial context of patient problems in reaching a diagnosis of the problem. In other words symptoms do not necessarily indicate a biological, pathological lesion.

● Symptoms and pathology
Further support for a different view of symptoms than that advanced by a strictly biomedical model comes from a variety of sources.

Screening for symptoms

In an attempt to uncover some of the 'clinical iceberg' in the community, medicine has devised screening programmes through which to identify previously unrecognized diseases. Sometimes these screening exercises have involved checking for symptoms as indicators of underlying pathology – the implication being, as in traditional biomedicine, that the symptom is present because a disease is also present. To check this assumption epidemiologists usually check the validity of finding the symptom (the screening test) by comparing it with more certain evidence for the existence of the disease (the reference test).

In trying to determine the extent of urinary tract infections in women in the community it is possible to use the presence of dysuria (pain or a burning sensation on micturition), one of the classic symptoms of urinary tract infection, as the screening test. Would this be adequate? The answer can be found by comparing the results of this screening test with the results of a reference test, namely the presence of bacteria in a midstream urine sample (MSU).

When the results of such a symptom check are linked with the results of the pathological test, an interesting picture emerges (Komaroff, 1984). First there are, of course, some patients who experience dysuria and who have a positive MSU and who therefore can be said to have urinary tract infection, and those patients with neither symptoms nor bacteria. On the other hand, somewhat surprisingly, there are some patients who experience the symptoms of urinary tract infection, but whose urine is sterile. The exact origins of the pain on micturition are unclear, but it would not appear to be due to urinary tract infection. And then there are those patients who are asymptomatic, experiencing no dysuria, yet who have positive MSU results. In other words these women have the bacteria of a urinary tract infection yet experience no symptoms.

How are these results to be interpreted? There may be some laboratory failings, but the magnitude of the picture suggests something else is happening. The classical medical model would suggest there should be a close correlation between symptoms and the pathological findings of disease. But in studies of the prevalence of urinary tract infections it would appear that there are considerably more women with only one of the dyad than with both. In these circumstances it is difficult to say whether, in fact, the women really have a disease as the exact nature of the disease is uncertain.

The implications of this for the medical model is that the supposed correlation between symptoms and pathology is not as clear-cut as it might seem. For example, patients may experience an anginal type of chest pain, yet on arterial cardiography show no narrowing of the coronary arteries. Have these patients got angina? Technically, no, because they have no narrowing of their coronaries. And yet they still experience the symptoms of the disease. So what, exactly, does the symptom mean if it occurs independently of underlining pathological change? It does at least suggest that the traditional biomedical model which would relate all symptoms to pathological change is inadequate for explaining the phenomenon.

The weakness of the biomedical model in these situations is not merely a theoretical one in that it does have real implications. For example, a third of patients with angina waiting for coronary artery surgery have psychiatric morbidity before the operation; after, these patients remain disturbed, and their angina and exercise tolerance improves less than in those patients without psychiatric illness beforehand (Channer *et al.*, 1988). To put it bluntly, a surgical operation to change a patient's anatomy is unlikely to be effective if the problem is not located in that anatomy.

●   Biographical medicine

Many general practitioners have observed that their patients have the symptoms of diseases, as described above, yet on investigation have no apparent pathology. This not uncommon situation has led many general practitioners to think about the nature of their work and the nature of illness. One famous attempt to understand what was happening was that provided by Michael Balint (1964). He was trained in both biomedicine and psychoanalysis and attempted to combine the two. He recognized that many of the problems presented by patients in general practice did not have an organic basis, despite mimicking traditional organic disease. He concluded from this that illness was a psychosocial phenomenon as much as a biological one and that this perspective had several important implications for the general practitioner's role.

1. First the general practitioner's task was not to diagnose and treat biological disease, but 'to organize unorganized illness'. Patients presented with disorganized illness: they had abdominal pain, they had domestic problems, they had experienced a severe life event. The doctor's task in these circumstances was to organize these disparate elements into a coherent picture which would explain the patient's experiences. This may have involved treating the abdominal pain – even with traditional biomedical therapy – but this was only a component of the overall diagnosis and treatment of the problem.
2. Balint also felt that traditional therapeutics was limited. Drugs to change the biological functioning of the body seemed of limited applicability given that very often the problem was not biological in nature. Besides it is well known that 50% of patients do not comply with the drugs given by the doctor; indeed perhaps 20% of patients do not even cash the prescription the doctor gives them. In the light of this, Balint argued that the most powerful therapeutic tool the doctor possessed was him or herself. Patients came to the doctor to get a 'dose of doctor'. In simple terms this can be seen as a sort of placebo, but the doctor had to recognize that it was not the technical medication but the human relationship which had the most effect on patients' welfare. Balint also pointed out that this drug, doctor, was relatively unexplored: no one knew of the correct dosages, of its addictive properties or of its side effects.
3. The third facet of general practice that Balint identified was the mutual investment that doctor and patient placed in their relationship. A consultation in general practice was not a single episode in which doctor treated the disease. The single consultation was simply one in a series of consultations which occurred over a lifetime. In other words each consultation followed on from the next in a sort of 'extended' consultation. And as the doctor got to know more and more about the patients, their biography, their relationships, their context, he or she was better able to use the time of each new consultation more effectively and develop a greater insight into the patient's needs.

At the same time, the consultation and this developing relationship also afforded an opportunity to develop insight into the doctor's own needs. In other words the relationship between doctor and patient was a mutual investment which, over time, should benefit both.

Balint's ideas were received sympathetically by many general practitioners who were aware of some of the complex reasons why patients consulted with them. They also knew that the scope for using the classical biomedical model was more limited in general practice than in hospitals because of the very different morbidity spectrum. For example, the average general practitioner will see 600 cases of upper respiratory tract infection a year (of which most are viral), 375 cases with non-specific symptoms, two cases of lung cancer (the commonest cancer), and one case of phenylketonuria every 200 years (Fry, 1983).

● Alternative models of illness

There is a growing demand for alternative therapies. Patients now seem much more willing to explore and use healing systems which use different underlying models of illness such as homoeopathy, acupuncture, osteopathy, etc. The reasons for this are no doubt various, but one of the factors seeming to influence this demand is the failure of biomedicine to address the full impact that illnesses have on patients. Traditional biomedicine simply addresses the pathological lesion whereas illness affects the whole patient. If the doctor therefore limits his or her focus, the patient is likely to be dissatisfied and to seek help elsewhere.

● Models of the doctor–patient relationship

The link with biomedicine

Jewson (1976) argues that the relationship between doctor and patient has a very close correspondence with the model of illness which dominates at any time. In the eighteenth century physicians were few in number and their patients mainly upper class and aristocratic. This status difference ensured a patient dominance in the doctor–patient relationship such that doctors had to compete amongst each other to please the patient. The model of illness that emerged from this relationship was one based on the complex interpretation of individual symptoms: doctors had no need to examine their patients, they only had to be attentive to their patients' demands and experiences (in the form of symptoms). The frequent use of this symptom-based model of illness, in its turn, ensured the maintenance of patient dominance in the doctor–patient relationship.

In the late eighteenth century the hospital emerged as a place to treat the poor sick, initially in Paris, then later throughout Europe. Doctors now found themselves treating (usually for charity) socially inferior and therefore more passive patients. Jewson argues that out of these social relations a new medicine emerged which stressed not the symptom, but the accurate diagnosis of a pathological lesion deep inside the body. This new biomedical model of illness required only the presence of the patient's body and the clinico-anatomical knowledge of the doctor. In short, the new medicine emerged out of a relationship between a dominant doctor and a passive patient, and the practice of the new medicine, in its turn, reproduced precisely this relationship between doctor and patient.

Consensual models

The biomedical model of illness and its related model of the appropriate doctor–patient relationship dominated the practice of medicine almost exclusively until the 1950s. The dominance of biomedicine can be seen in any contemporary text on clinical method (Armstrong, 1984), and the particular relationship which was viewed as appropriate can be seen in Parsons' formulation of the sick role which was described in the wider context of understanding relationships in modern society (1951). The notion of the sick role was advanced to explain the formal network of mutual obligations and expectations that exists between doctor and patient (see Chapter 2). The doctor has a role which involves acting in the patient's medical interests; the patient's role was defined in terms of four, now well-known, specific characteristics:

(i)   the patient gains temporary exemption from normal role responsibilities;
(ii) the patient is not held responsible for his or her own illness;
(iii) the patient must want to get well;
(iv) the patient should comply with legitimate medical advice.

Although there are some carrots in this relationship for the patient, the dominant picture to emerge is of a relatively passive and obedient patient; this would seem fully in accord with the requirements of the biomedical model.

By the late 1950s, however, particularly under the influence of psychoanalytic theories, a new dimension to illness – in the form of recognition of a psychological aspect – began to appear. It can be seen in the Balint view of general practice, outlined above, but also in a well-known typology of different forms of the doctor–patient relationship published in 1956.

Szasz and Hollender suggested that three types of doctor–patient relationship could be identified:

1. Activity–passivity: in which the doctor is active and the patient is a passive recipient of medical treatment and advice.
2. Cooperation–guidance: where the doctor guides the patient, who cooperates.
3. Mutual participation: where both doctor and patient negotiate and share the crucial decisions.

Szasz and Hollender likened these types to different stages of childhood. Activity–passivity is equivalent to the relationship between a parent and a baby. The baby is wholly dependent on the parent for everything. The cooperation–guidance is more akin to a child and parent in which the child can respond yet must still rely on the overall guidance of the parent. Finally, mutual participation is said to mirror that of a relationship between adults: in this both participants are autonomous and equal.

Conflict models

Both Parsons' and Szasz and Hollender's models share a consensual approach: both doctor and patient have a common agenda because it is still ultimately the biomedical view which predominates. True, Szasz and Hollender preferred mutual participation, but they assumed that this would be achieved in the context of a shared belief in the biomedical model. Yet all the while the new psychosocial dimensions were being explored and with them a realization that the traditional consensus between doctor and patient was not inviolable. The interests of doctor and patient could diverge and the doctor's biomedical interest in the patient's disease may not be entirely the same as the patient's interest in the wider impact of the disease on their lives. This led various sociologists in the 1970s to propose a 'conflict' model of doctor–patient interaction in which competing perspectives could be acknowledged.

Freidson (1970) offered a broad critique of conventional doctor–patient explanations, pointing out that despite their apparent belief in consensus, they were all doctor-centred. In other words the relationship was seen entirely in terms of what the doctor had to achieve, namely biomedical diagnosis and treatment. Instead, Freidson argued there was a fundamental clash of perspectives between doctor and patient. For the doctor the patient was simply another clinical case in a long stream. For the patient, on the other hand, the illness was a very personal experience which was unique. These different perspectives led to potential conflict. Indeed Freidson pointed out that the three types of doctor–patient relationship described by Szasz and Hollender were logically incomplete. If the doctor could have three roles, active, guiding and participating, then so too could the patient. This led him to propose the addition of two further 'types' to the original list. These were, guidance–cooperation, in which the patient guided the doctor who cooperated, and passivity–activity where the doctor was passive and the patient active. In other words the leadership in the consultation could fall to either doctor or patient.

Negotiation models

In recent years the limitations of the traditional biomedical model have become more apparent. This realization, together with the knowledge that patients have complex lay theories which they bring to the doctor, points to any conflict in the doctor–patient relationship being really over models of illness. Put simply, the doctor has a biomedical view of illness, and the patient has a psychosocial one derived from their experience.

Many doctors, recognizing this inherent conflict, have turned to wider models of illness and adopted new strategies in the consultation, particularly those which try and elicit the patient's views so that these perspectives can be addressed. Nevertheless, there is evidence that for many consultations the doctors' narrow construction of the nature of the medical illness causes them to lose sight of the problems presented by the patient. For example, in a detailed study of 328 consultations between general practitioners and their patients in England, patients were interviewed after the consultation and asked what they could recall of what had happened and the advice given (Tuckett et al., 1985). It was found that patients were by and large able to remember the key points that the doctor made about the diagnosis, its significance and the appropriate action to be taken. However, while the key points could be remembered, fewer patients could actually make correct sense – as the doctor intended – of the consultation. And when it came to looking at whether the patients were actually committed to the key points the doctor had made, the proportion of patients fell to about two-thirds. In other words a third of the patients, while being able to recall what the doctor had said, did not feel that the doctor's advice fitted the nature of the problem as they saw it.

These different models of the doctor–patient relationship and their evolution suggest that the nature of the relationship is intimately bound up with the way that illness is defined. As this chapter has shown, re-emphasizing points already made in previous chapters, illness can be construed in a variety of ways. Traditionally biomedicine has been the dominant way of interpreting illness, that is reducing it to a pathological lesion, and expecting compliance from patients. Increasingly this view is seen to be too limited, and certainly would not appear to be entirely congruent with the patient's own interests, in which even non-compliance with medical advice may be a means of illness management on the part of the patient (Conrad, 1985). The route to a satisfied patient would seem to be to address these wider aspects of illness.

● References

Armstrong, D. (1984) The patient's view. *Social Science and Medicine,* **18**, 737–744

Balint, M. (1964) *The Doctor, His Patient and the Illness,* Pitman, London

Brown, G. W. and Harris, T. (1978) *Social Origins of Depression,* Tavistock, London

Channer, K. S., O'Connor, S., Britton, S. *et al.* (1988) Psychological factors influence the success of coronary artery surgery. *Journal of the Royal Society of Medicine,* **81**, 629–632

Conrad, P. (1985) The meaning of medicalisation: another look at compliance. *Social Science and Medicine,* **20**, 29–37

Craig, T. K. and Brown, G. W. (1984) Goal frustrating aspects of life event stress in the aetiology of gastrointestinal disorder. *Journal of Psychosomatic Research,* **28**, 411–421

Creed, F. H. (1981) Life events and appendicectomy. *Lancet,* **i**, 1381–1385

Freidson, E. (1970) *Profession of Medicine,* Dodd Mead, New York,

Fry, J. (1983) *Present State and Future Needs in General Practice,* MTP Press, Lancaster

Jewson, N. K. (1976) Disappearance of the sick-man from medical cosmologies, 1770–1870. *Sociology,* **10**, 225–244

Komaroff, A. L. (1984) Acute dysuria in women. *New England Journal of Medicine,* **310**, 368–375

Meyer, R. J. and Haggerty, R. J. (1962) Streptococcal infection in families: factors altering individual susceptibility. *Pediatrics,* **29**, 539–549

Parsons, T. (1951) *The Social System,* Free Press, New York

Szasz, T. S. and Hollender, M. H. (1956) A contribution to the philosophy of medicine: the basic models of the doctor patient relationship. *Archives of Internal Medicine,* **97**, 585–592

Tuckett, D., Boulton, M., Olson, C. *et al.* (1985) *Meetings Between Experts: An Approach to Sharing Ideas in Medical Consultations,* Tavistock, London

Turner, R. M. (1978) Recurrent abdominal pain in childhood. *Journal of the Royal College of General Practitioners,* **28**, 729–734

10

Types of health care

Symptoms and illness as has been shown in Chapter 2 are very common in the community. In deciding on appropriate treatment patients have a choice of possibilities ranging from dealing with the symptoms themselves to obtaining professional help.

• Self-care

Given the quantity of symptoms and illness experienced by people it is apparent that most are treated by self-care. Most patients have knowledge of how to treat common conditions: a bruise, a cut, a headache, a bad cold, etc. They supplement these skills with various pharmacological preparations. It has been shown that the average household in Britain contains about ten different medicines (Dunnell and Cartwright, 1972). Some of these have been prescribed by doctors in the past, and some have been obtained as over the counter medicines from the local pharmacist. These resources are widely used (Anderson, 1979). There is evidence to suggest that people take, on average, at least two different medicines every week. Some studies have suggested that self-medication is so high that in any 24-hour period about half the population will have swallowed some pharmacological preparation.

Some people, who could look after themselves when ill, choose to use the health services instead. They therefore consume resources which could be devoted to people more in need. This logic has influenced health services – and the agencies which ultimately foot the bill – to encourage more self-care. This strategy seems particularly important when it comes to prevention because if people could be persuaded to follow healthy activities then this should diminish morbidity in the future.

Using a strategy to improve self-care, particularly in the field of preventive activity, has clear advantages both for people's health and for the future costs of health services. There are, however, two major problems which can arise if this policy is pursued too enthusiastically.

1. If people are persuaded to take responsibility for their health, there can be an unforeseen cost if they fail because, in a sense, they are then responsible for their illness. This outcome has been called 'victim-blaming' because the victims of illness, instead of receiving sympathy and support, are offered

blame (Crawford, 1977). Victim-blaming is a particular problem for lower socio-economic groups as they are least likely to be able to 'look after' their health for reasons discussed in earlier chapters.

2. The related problem with giving people responsibility for their own health is that many individual measures are ineffective in the face of socio-structural causes of ill health such as social class, poverty, unemployment, etc. Moreover, an emphasis on the supposed value of individual measures deflects attention from both wider social deprivation and other problems onto the individual (Kronenfeld, 1979).

● Family care

While many people cope with illnesses by themselves they also draw upon the resources of those living around them, often of necessity. These people can offer support and advice and a form of lay nursing if required. Most childhood illnesses, for example, are treated in this way.

The family unit

Obtaining help and support from those living around usually means depending on the family unit. However, examining the extent and effectiveness of such family support depends on defining the family. On the one hand it is all too 'familiar', and forms the basic building blocks of our society; on the other hand it turns out that this familiarity is more than likely founded on a rather mythical idealized family unit. How then can the nature of families be explored?

Historical origins

It was a common belief until a few years ago that society before the Industrial Revolution was characterized by the *extended family* which involved various relatives, beyond mother, father and children, living together in the same household. This pattern of family life was supposed to have given way in modern times to the *nuclear family* which encompasses only parents and their immediate offspring.

This view of a historical transition between two types of family structure misrepresents the past as well as the present. Various historical demographic studies have shown that the nuclear family, far from being only a relatively recent development, was common in pre-industrial societies (Anderson, 1980). Moreover it would appear from studies of some traditional working class communities that, while perhaps not restricted to the same dwelling place, the ties and interaction of the extended family have formed a major part of community life to the present day.

Current structure

The typical modern family is usually held to be mother, father and dependent children. However from Table 10.1 it can be seen that, if the current pattern of household formation in the UK is examined, then the so-called typical family does scant justice to the evidence. First, only about three-quarters of households can be described as family-based in that there are relatives living together. Of these about one-third are composed of a married couple without dependent children. A half of all households contain children but many of these only have a single parent.

Table 10.1. Households in Britain. (After OPCS, 1989)

	%
One person	
Over retirement age	16
Under retirement age	9
Two or more unrelated adults	3
Married couple	
No children	27
With dependent children	28
With non-dependent children	9
Lone parent	
With dependent children	4
With non-dependent children	4
Two or more families	1
	———
	100%

Average household size = 2.55 people

It would seem, therefore, that it is difficult to generalize about the family simply because there is no such thing as a standard family (particularly as even within the same apparent family structure, relationships can vary so much). For many analyses the household is a more useful measure than the family whatever its apparent familiarity.

Family sentiment
It is often assumed that the family in the past was characterized by the same sort of roles and forms of interaction as it is today. Historical work on the family, however, has argued the provocative case that the affect and sentiment which is part of modern family life was absent in the past and relationships were founded more on economic and formal bonds. If this argument is correct then it would appear that the expectations and benefits of family life have changed considerably over the years.

The reason for stressing this changing nature of family life is for the light it can shed on the interpretation of the contemporary family and its relationship to health. Take a well-known 'problem' of family life, such as the rising divorce rate: does this signify the decline of family life or perhaps indicate its strengthening? On the one hand the divorce rate can be seen as an indicator of marriage failure and, as it is increasing, marriage might seem more parlous than years ago.

Alternatively, inasmuch as the rising divorce rate tends to follow changes in the law which make divorce easier, it is possible that marriages which had already broken down are now being decently legally interred. On the other hand if, as suggested above, the affective bonds which characterize family life are growing stronger, then the expectations of family life in terms of emotional support and security may similarly be increasing. When a partner finds that the relationship fails to provide this support then, rather than remain within a poor relationship, he or she chooses to seek a better alternative. In effect a rising divorce rate may represent stronger family ties and commensurate higher standards in evaluating them. It is noteworthy that most people who leave a marriage are, within a few years, remarried. *t often little divorce*

Insofar as health is concerned it would appear that the family may be of little explanatory value because of the diversity of its forms; more useful might be the *household* as the basic demographic unit and *social support* as the most important aspect of family functioning.

Availability of family care

Whether family-based care is provided in illness depends on the ability and willingness of household members to take on the task. In addition, family members may be required to take on care if the health care system fails to provide. The main role of the formal health care system is to care for people whose illnesses are too difficult and too serious to be managed solely within the home; but this demarcation is dependent on the adequacy of resources in both formal and household sectors. On the one hand, resources within the health care system are rarely adequate completely to cover all who need such care so that many people with serious and debilitating conditions must 'cope' at home, perhaps with the help of a close relative. On the other hand, facilities, skills and support may be lacking in the home. Many ill people, especially the elderly, who might benefit from care by their immediate families, are unable to obtain it because they either do not live in a 'family unit' or have people available who might be in a position to offer care. In these circumstances the patient must be either accepted into hospital (often as a so-called 'social admission') or found a place within another institution, such as an old people's home or nursing home, which can provide the resources and care that the patient's own home lacks.

Costs of family care

Having an ill person in the home can lead to extra expense: heating, lighting, cleaning, food, shopping, special facilities, etc. These additional costs which would otherwise be carried by insurance or hospitals are placed on families which look after their ill at home.

The largest additional cost, however, is more difficult to quantify and relates to the problems involved in finding someone within the family actually to do the caring. One of the traditional tasks for women, besides running the home, was to look after members of the family who fell ill (women themselves not being expected to become ill). However, with the changing role of women in contemporary society, more having full-time jobs, perhaps more sharing of domestic tasks, it can be difficult to find someone actually to do the caring. Who should take time off work? Who should get up at night? What costs in terms of added tensions and friction within the home are incurred?

One of the problems is that we know so little about care in the home, its costs and its benefits. In many situations it might well be the best treatment; in others it might be inappropriate for either the well-being of the patient or domestic harmony. Medical trials of 'home' versus 'hospital' treatment for various problems rarely attempt to evaluate these costs on the family. Despite our ignorance of the extent and limits of informal care it would be wrong to take it for granted.

- **Community care**

The value of family and household care for many illnesses is clear but, as pointed out above, such care can place great burdens on the family, and it assumes the existence of family members in some ideal setting who are willing and able to take on full caring functions. It is apparent that for many illnesses these cannot be assumed. But in the absence of family care great demands would be made on health care services. Thus the policy of many countries is to encourage home care, and support it with more resources from the formal health care system on a community basis: hence an emphasis on 'community care'.

The idea of community care emerged in the 1950s, particularly in response to the discharge of patients from large mental hospitals. In effect, community care then meant care *in* the community (in contrast to care in an institution). In recent years, however, the term has come to mean *by* the community as the resources of the latter have been mobilized to help.

With adequate resources general practitioners can manage more health problems in the community without the patient being hospitalized. The community or district nurse can treat problems in the patient's own home which would otherwise have required hospital nursing care. Provision of home helps to look after domestic chores or meals-on-wheels to provide food can supplement home resources. Grants and benefits to those willing to stay at home and look after aged and incapacitated relatives can prevent such people from being permanently institutionalized. And so on.

These attempts to bolster the power of informal care to look after more people in the community might be welcomed on the basis that home care is generally preferable to the anonymity of hospital care. However several criticisms of community care have been made which deserve consideration.

1. Community care is often under-funded. To a certain extent formal and informal health care systems are complementary such that if one system defaults the other tends to compensate. This apparent reciprocity between the systems, it has been argued, has been seized on by governments intent on reducing expenditure on formal health care services. The most expensive feature of hospital and institutional care is the hotel costs. Keeping a patient in bed and providing him with services such as cleaning, heating, lighting, food, etc. is very expensive and if these costs can be removed by caring for the person in his own home in the community then considerable savings result. Thus it is possible to dispense with expensive hospital-based services by giving a vague and perhaps token commitment to community care. But what in fact happens is that the increased resources going to community care are wholly inadequate and it is left to the family and individuals to pick up the pieces. Poor funding over many years also means that health professionals, skilled in community care, are in short supply.
2. Community care requires coordination and collaboration between various health and welfare agencies which often does not exist; nor is it clear who should be responsible for organizing coordination.
3. Professional interests tend to support the status quo, especially the preeminence of hospital funding. Encouraging of community care usually means the reallocation of resources away from the hospital sector, and for this reason is often resisted.
4. Community care, by the community, depends on the willingness and ability of the community to cope. The burden usually falls on families, particularly

women in those families (see above). The role of women has been changing rapidly and it is becoming increasingly unreasonable to expect wives and daughters to devote themselves full time to the care of other members of the family unit.

The major difficulty with community care is therefore that it might produce a net saving and reduction in government spending but a comparable (and hidden) additional cost falling on families with illness. Costs are therefore removed from the whole community (in terms of government expenditure) and placed on individual families with the illnesses who may well be the least able to bear the increased demands.

Commitment to community care must therefore be seen in the context of who pays the costs – in all their forms – for this service. Community care, when adequately provided, is a very different phenomenon from when it over-relies on the informal care system – which might well be weighed down with its own problems anyway.

● Self-help groups

Some diseases and illnesses pose particular problems for care. These problems may be of a material nature, for example, the illness may be physically disabling, or there may be a need for psychological support. Health professions and lay people provide treatment and help, but sometimes not of the right kind. This has led some patients with particular illnesses which produce very particular needs, to group together to form their own communities of self-help groups. A self-help group enables the patient to obtain support and advice from others with similar conditions. For many diseases and for many patients this seems to be very important (Robinson and Henry, 1977).

Self-help groups might be seen as meeting health service deficiencies. For example the doctor treats multiple sclerosis as a particular debilitating disease, but for the patient who has to live with it 24 hours a day it is an overwhelming experience. Sharing this experience with others with the disease seems to be very helpful, both in terms of advice on physical problems and emotional support. Equally sharing experiences of the disease can be seen as a sort of protest movement against the biomedical model which reduces illness to a pathological lesion. In multiple sclerosis, colostomy, epilepsy, diabetes, etc. the disease is more than the biological deficit, and self-help groups enable the illness in its wider context to be made salient and for help and support to be provided.

Self-help groups, from their early beginnings, have often been very successful. Their membership can number many thousands, and they often produce newsletters and hold meetings for their members. Over the years some groups have been so successful that they have begun to organize themselves on more bureaucratic lines. They appoint a director, have a formal constitution, and raise funds for themselves and for research into their condition. The group comes to have specialized knowledge about the particular disease which very few doctors, if any, are likely to have; and self-help groups in sponsoring research become influential in guiding treatment priorities.

As the process of acquiring expertise develops, the self-help group starts to become a rival to the skills and knowledge of doctors, and this situation can lead to an ambivalent relationship with the medical profession. In part this may be because the self-help group begins to recruit doctors to the organization for advice and help. But this immediately compromises the characteristic of the self-help group as a form of alternative medicine. Indeed it is possible that the self-help group may be simply taken over by doctors and used as an extension of the health care system. These tensions are usually resolved in different ways. Some self-help groups become incorporated into medicine with a major medical dominance. Others choose to remain wholly independent of medicine, keeping their autonomy, yet losing any benefits that medicine might confer. Yet others exist in the tension between these two strategies: the medical profession is seen to be part of the solution, yet it is also part of the problem.

● Professional care

Professional care might be defined as that health care delivered by people in part or full time employment in a health care capacity. There are various subdivisions of professional care which can be made.

Primary versus secondary

Most health services have evolved a system of specialization in which there are experts in particular types of illness. This has clear advantages for patients in that they can find someone with particular expertise of relevance to their problem. However, there are two problems with specialization in medicine: first, there has to be a mechanism to ensure that patients and their problems are steered to the right specialist (as the patients themselves are unlikely to know the appropriate person), and second, it would be prohibitively expensive to treat all illnesses, especially minor ones, with specialist resources. This has led health care to be split between primary and secondary services.

Primary care
Primary care is provided for patients at first contact with the health service. By its very nature it must be generalist, being able to cope with whatever problems arise. General practitioners are the traditional primary care doctors, though in recent years they are increasingly becoming a part of a primary care team, involving a wider range of health professionals and their respective skills.

If the problem warrants it, the patient can be transferred from the primary sector to the hospital-based secondary sector. In the USA many doctors perform both roles, being primary care physicians and specialists in some branch of hospital medicine. This means the distinction between sectors is sometimes blurred. In the UK, on the other hand, for historical reasons (Honigsbaum, 1979) there is a fairly rigid demarcation between general practice and hospital. This manifests itself in much less cross-over between the two for doctors (who will rarely follow their patients into hospital) and a rule that, except for emergencies, patients' only access to the secondary sector is through the general practitioner. In the USA patients are at liberty to go directly to a specialist or a hospital if they choose; in the UK they must be referred by their general practitioner. As the secondary sector is much more expensive than the primary, this tends to mean lower health costs in the UK, other things being equal.

The idea that good primary health care is an effective and cheap means of managing most illnesses has not been lost on financially pressed health care systems. There is now general encouragement for doctors to go into primary health care, and there is a greater flow of resources into the sector to enable more and more illnesses to be treated in this way. Indeed the World Health

Organization, in its blueprint for 'Health for All by the Year 2000' places special emphasis on primary health care services, particularly in developing countries in which funding is even more limited.

This recent emphasis on the importance of primary health care has further improved its status in the medical world. From being the sieve which separated out the 'interesting' cases for the hospital, general practice has increasingly become a special type of medicine in its own right, often with its own distinctive models of illness (Armstrong, 1979).

Secondary care

Specialist services usually require access to beds and, often, expensive equipment: it therefore tends to be based in hospitals. On occasion its technology is so complex and its knowledge base so esoteric that some of it is sometimes given a label of tertiary care. It is, above all, expensive, and in recent years has been the focus of various strategies of cost containment (see Chapters 11 and 12).

Orthodox versus unorthodox

There has always been a struggle between orthodox and unorthodox healers. The orthodox, of course, is simply that group which has managed to seize the high ground – in Western medicine for the last 200 years that means biomedicine. The unorthodox are those healers who somehow are sufficiently different to pose a potential threat to the orthodox.

Orthodoxy protects its interests with two strategies, namely marginalization and incorporation. Marginalization means that rival practitioners are excluded from regular medical work by labelling them as charlatans. Thus the 1858 legislation in the UK which gave a legal basis to the medical profession's right to practise medicine excluded many healers who used non-biomedical approaches.

In recent years the medical profession has seemed to show a more liberal view of unorthodox healers. Does this mean they are becoming more tolerant? Or is it a change in strategy? Perhaps because these alternative medicines have public support, it has been judged wiser to try and neutralize them through incorporating them into medicine than allowing them the possibility of further independent growth. There is now the interesting spectacle of biomedical practitioners carrying out acupuncture, homoeopathy, etc. though often in a manner not approved of by alternative practitioners themselves.

Private versus public

There is a distinction between health services bought in a private negotiation between doctor and patient, and health services provided as a right, free at the point of use. However, in most countries of the world this distinction is becoming increasingly blurred as different political ideologies jostle for influence over health care provision. These issues are dealt with in Chapter 12.

Teamwork versus solo practice

Increasingly health care is provided by groups of health care professionals; in these teams the doctor is only one member. Efficient teamwork depends on good personal relations and a clear definition of what each member's responsibilities are. The professional aspirations of team members, however, can create various tensions. First, occupational groups such as nurses and other paramedical groups are trying to achieve some autonomy from medicine, and this can lead to rivalries and ill feeling. Second, because the new professional groups are trying to carve out a specific knowledge area there can be clashes between neighbouring groups as to who possesses expertise in a certain situation.

Who for example should take charge of caring for chronically ill people in the community? General practitioners, social workers, health visitors, district nurses, etc. all have a claim to lead the health care team. But each of these groups has a different knowledge base which at times overlaps with other members of the team, and at other times produces a different set of priorities and definitions of the situation.

● **References**

Anderson, J. A. D. (ed.) (1979) *Self-Medication,* MTP Press, Lancaster

Anderson, M. (1980) *Approaches to the History of the Western Family: 1500–1914.* Macmillan, London

Armstrong, D. (1979) The emancipation of biographical medicine. *Social Science and Medicine,* **13**, 1–8

Crawford, R. (1977) You are dangerous to your health: the ideology and politics of victim-blaming. *International Journal of Health Services,* **7**, 663–679

Dunnell, K. and Cartwright, A. (1972) *Medicine Takers, Prescribers and Hoarders,* Routledge and Kegan Paul, London

Honigsbaum, F. (1979) *The Division in British Medicine,* Kogan Page, London

Kronenfeld, J. J. (1979) Self-care as panacea for the ills of the health care system: an assessment. *Social Science and Medicine,* **13A**, 263–267

Robinson, D. and Henry, S. (1977) *Self-Help and Health.* Martin Robertson, London

11

Clinical autonomy

One meaning of the term 'professional' simply means paid; it is the opposite of amateur. But those occupations known as professions also have a more important social significance.

When sociologists first studied the nature of professional groups in the 1950s they concluded that the professions offered a type of service which was quite distinct from that of other occupations (Goode, 1960). Doctors were seen as an archetypal profession and their work had certain key features. One was an esoteric knowledge base: in other words they had very specialized knowledge which patients needed. Another was a service ideal, that is a commitment to the patient that went beyond the simply financial. The three great professions of medicine, the law and the church fitted this description well. Practitioners in each of these professions possessed specialized knowledge which was not easily accessible to lay people, and in addition they professed to be more interested in their client's welfare than in their own.

In retrospect it is now thought that sociological studies of the period too readily accepted the professions' own claims to expertise and altruism. A new more sceptical analysis of professions emerged in the 1970s which argued that these claims to a service ideal and esoteric knowledge were simply devices for ensuring the success of the professional groups themselves (Johnson, 1972).

The cornerstone of professional status now seems to rest with the control they have achieved over the content of their work (Freidson, 1970). In the case of doctors this means that they have 'clinical autonomy'. On the one hand, it does seem important that doctors are given sufficient freedom from external constraint to make judgements and direct resources in their patients' interests. On the other hand, this lack of accountability has some dangers both in the power it gives the doctor to decide what is in the best interests of the patient (without necessary regard for their views) and in the ability to allocate large amounts of public resources without being answerable to any management structure.

In recent years this lack of accountability that the medical profession has traditionally enjoyed has been challenged in a variety of ways. In each case the strategy seems to be to achieve a careful balance between allowing clinical autonomy as far as possible – because doctors must be permitted certain freedoms in their clinical work – and constraining their ability to allocate large amounts of resources.

- ## Controlling information

The power of the medical profession to claim to work without supervision and accountability rests with their specialized knowledge. A hospital manager cannot tell a physician who to treat with a certain drug, nor would it appear easy to reprimand a surgeon for operating unnecessarily without specialized surgical knowledge. Knowledge and skill is therefore an essential feature of professional autonomy.

Training

One means of influencing the medical profession is through their training: if doctors are trained to act in a certain, cost-effective way, then it seems a reasonable hope that they will continue to do so throughout their professional lives. The problem is that medical education has traditionally been controlled by the profession itself, so the opportunity for external bodies such as governments to influence it has been limited. Nevertheless, governments usually control various aspects of funding, both in the training itself and in setting research priorities, which in their turn can influence the knowledge and emphases of medical education. Therefore the potential is present for some direct intervention into the training of doctors, both in medical school and in specialist training, though as yet the opportunity has been little used in a self-conscious way.

More used has been the ability of governments to control the accreditation and licensing of doctors. In the USA, states often control preliminary licensing, together with regular requirements for further and continuing education. In the UK, most education is controlled by the profession but government influence is increasing. There is now a statutory requirement, for example, to complete three years training before being eligible to be a general practitioner. In this way governments must hope that more education and specialty training will produce more effective and efficient doctors.

Information flows

One of the arguments against clinical autonomy is that not only are doctors not accountable to anyone for their allocation of resources, but they are often ignorant of how much they are actually spending. The doctor decides a patient needs a blood test, an operation, or a drug, and then provides it without knowing how much it costs. Clearly, in certain situations a service must be provided irrespective of the cost (though this is not true for all services that are 'needed', especially the very expensive ones). But equally there are many situations in which, say, a particular test is not really necessary, or for which there is a cheaper alternative.

The argument follows that if doctors were made aware of the true costs of the services that they dispense, then they would be able to make more cost-effective clinical decisions. This has led to an increasing flow of information to doctors informing them of either the costs of decisions that they might make, or the costs of decisions that they have made. For example, British general practitioners are now supplied with monthly data on the numbers and costs of all their prescribing, together with comparative data for costs in their locality and nationally. Thus general practitioners are in a position to know whether their prescribing is above or below the norms set by their colleagues, the assumption being that those with high costs will feel guilty enough to change their prescribing habits.

But of course there are many reasons for expensive prescribing, and general practitioners can argue to themselves that their costs are justified. In other words, doctors do not have to respond to information; they do have to change, however, when faced by various more direct methods of cost containment.

● **Controlling costs**

Because of the uncertain nature of medical work, doctors cannot be told how much to spend on each patient. However, they can be given various overall constraints on expenditure.

Limited prescribing lists

Doctors need the freedom to prescribe the drugs which will benefit their patients. However, the costs of drugs to a health service is very high – more than 10% of total expenditure – and it is generally believed that in many instances doctors prescribe expensive drugs when a cheaper one would work just as effectively. In part this may be due to lack of knowledge of relative costs or of the similar pharmacological properties of a cheaper preparation; but in addition, a major part of continuing medical education is provided by the pharmaceutical industry, and it has a vested interest in persuading doctors to use expensive drugs while informing them of the benefits of its latest product.

Generic prescribing, in which only the generic drug names are used, would be considerably cheaper because for those drugs out of patent protection, the proprietary product is usually a lot more expensive. However, again with the support of the pharmaceutical industry, doctors have resisted this change on the grounds that it is an unwarranted intrusion into their clinical autonomy to prescribe what they consider is best for their patients.

One response to the cost of prescriptions has been to inform doctors of costs and relative pharmacological benefits. The other has been to limit the range of drugs that doctors are allowed to prescribe. Most hospitals now have limited prescribing lists in which only a restricted number of drugs are available. Certain drugs – either ineffective or for which there is a cheaper alternative – have been placed on a black list in general practice so that if general practitioners wish to prescribe them the patient must pay their full cost.

Some doctors have objected to these constraints as a threat to clinical freedom, but most doctors have quietly accepted the restrictions. Indeed doctors themselves have always been intimately involved in drawing up these lists, and critics can hardly argue a very powerful case in favour of ineffective therapies. Nevertheless many doctors see these limitations as the beginning of greater constraints on clinical freedom.

Diagnosis-related groups

In the USA health care costs have risen very rapidly (see Chapter 12). In response, a diagnosis-related group system of payment has been introduced for many services as a means of containing costs through restricting the doctor's ability to spend. The essence of the scheme is to limit the amount of payment to doctors and hospitals from the government and insurance companies on the basis of the patient's particular medical problem. This is done by dividing all medical problems into about 500 what are called diagnosis-related groups, or DRGs. For each particular DRG a fixed payment is made. This encourages both doctor and hospital to restrain their expenditure to the expected amount they will receive. Some allowance is made for the fact that medical problems are unpredictable by permitting some increase in payment if there are either complications or other co-existing medical problems. However, to prevent providers making too many claims under these categories their number is strictly limited.

Faced with these constraints health care providers in the USA have pursued several strategies to try and minimize the effect of DRGs.

1. The practice of shifting diagnostic categories called 'DRG creep'. Hospitals and doctors have a bias towards making diagnoses on patients which carry a larger payment from the insurance body in terms of the DRG concerned. Thus, if a myocardial infarction carries a higher payment than angina, it is in the provider's interest to make the former diagnosis rather than the latter.
2. Since the payment which each DRG attracts is primarily based around length of bed stay in a hospital (this usually being the most expensive part of treatment), there is an incentive for early discharge of patients back to their homes and into the community. This, of course, simply shifts the costs of looking after illness from the hospital and/or doctor onto the community and the patient's own family.
3. The third problem of DRGs is it can lead to selection of patients. Certain DRGs are believed to offer underpayment and others overpayment. Thus diagnostic conditions which often overrun the agreed payment schedule will cause doctors and hospitals to run into losses. On the other hand DRGs which carry a relatively large payment in terms of the usual costs of treatment will enable doctor and hospital to make a profit. There is therefore an incentive to admit only those patients with particular diagnoses which are known to be covered by or to undershoot the appropriate DRG payment.

Clinical budgeting/management controls

The other more general way of cost-containment is some sort of control over total clinical expenditure. This can be effected in a variety of ways.

1. On a very general view, resources can be allocated to different geographical regions of a country on the basis of health need. Identifying health and health need is difficult (see Chapter 3), but after considering the various options the British NHS used mortality as the best available measure (DHSS, 1976). The Resource Allocation Working Party (RAWP) which made the choice suggested that resources should be allocated on the basis of a four-part formula:
   (a) population size;
   (b) corrected for age and sex;
   (c) an allowance for cross-boundary flows across neighbouring geographical regions;
   (d) standardized mortality ratio.

The overall result was a reallocation of resources away from the relatively well off south of the country to the north. Doctors in those geographical areas which lost resources, or at least who failed to benefit, found themselves severely constrained in the money they could spend on their patients.

2. Application of the RAWP formula created a more difficult resource environment for whole areas of the country. But if there were to be cost savings some of these had to fall on specific specialties. Thus another way of constraining expenditure is for health service managers to place a ceiling on spending in an attempt to bring high cost departments under some sort of control. Doctors are told at the beginning of the year that there is a fixed budget available for their services. When, and if, they reach that limit during the year they simply have to stop seeing more patients and incurring additional expenditure.

This is a fairly blunt weapon, and seems of dubious efficiency. Certainly cost thresholds are not breached, but expensive fixed costs – such as salaries – still have to be paid even though health care staff may be in enforced idleness. When health service resources are limited it does seem foolish to waste some resources as a means of constraining expenditure elsewhere in the system.

3. Another more sophisticated strategy of imposing a spending ceiling is to impose a maximum limit to expenditure, but then give control of that budget directly to the doctors concerned. The doctors then become responsible for how that money is spent.

Giving doctors direct responsibility for budgeting can be effective. First, they have far better information on costs, so they are potentially able to make more cost-effective decisions. Second, because they have control of allocations they are better able to distribute the money over the required time period without running out at the end. Third, involving doctors increases their commitment to the notion of cost control: it is not a faceless manager dictating to doctors, but a means of maintaining – even enhancing – their clinical autonomy.

The major difficulty with clinical budgeting is that it requires doctors partly to become managers as some of their time must be spent on financial management tasks. Besides the initial lack of skill and experience in this area, it means that doctors are drawn away from clinical work for an increased portion of their time. Doctors have had a highly specialized training in clinical work and it does seem inappropriate that at times they have to ignore their primary role and become amateur managers.

● Paying the doctor

Compared with the overall costs of providing health care, the cost of paying doctors (who number about 5% of all health service personnel) is relatively small. Few costs would therefore be saved by restraining medical earnings – though doctors pay no doubt forms a benchmark for other health service salaries. However, the method of paying the doctor does seem to have a major influence on health service expenditure, quite apart from the doctors' own pay, as well as on the type of service provided (Abel-Smith, 1976).

There are basically three methods of reimbursing the doctor and their relative advantages and disadvantages will be described, together with the influence they have on health costs and the definition of health need.

Fee-for-service

This is the usual method of payment in health care systems which tend to be dominated by 'private' funding and a market orientation (see Chapter 12). The doctor is paid a separate sum for each 'item' of service he or she provides. This method of payment is also found when insurance companies or governments intervene to cover patients for the costs of their care, the doctor charging them directly or indirectly for the services provided for insured patients.

The virtues of this system seem obvious. Doctors are paid, like many other skilled people, for the particular service they render. If they work hard, then they receive a commensurate increase in income; if they choose to work only two days a week then they receive accordingly less. In short, fee-for-service acts as an incentive for the doctors to work hard.

In manufacturing industry this piece-rate system may have much to commend it – the harder the labour force works the greater the output and the larger the workers' incomes. Yet in providing health care to individual patients, the doctor's keenness to work might actually be counter-productive. Many medical problems may require the doctor to wait or be vigilant rather than be committed to speedy or heroic intervention.

Thus while fee-for-service may be suitable for other occupations it does raise problems in medicine: given the doctor's claim to be able to identify health needs it is the doctor who judges which service is necessary (not the consumer as in other situations) and thereby decides whether to collect a fee or not. In short, the doctor comes to have a vested interest in illness rather than in health. Slight menorrhagia, for example, may be more likely to become justification for an operation if gynaecologists will be paid extra money than if they will not.

Although there are professional and ethical pressures to prevent financial criteria from affecting medical decision-making it has still proved necessary to organize widespread checks on medical practice when fee-for-service is the norm. In the USA, for example, peer review bodies will often assess the appropriateness of all surgery in a hospital and bring pressure to bear on those who seem to be 'over-operating'. Peer group assessment, however, suffers from the potential bias that evaluation by fellow surgeons might introduce. It is now well established that those health services or parts of health services which use fee-for-service, carry out more medical procedures, examinations, investigations, operations, etc. than those which do not.

Another example is afforded by the dental service within the NHS which mainly operates on a fee-for-service basis. Here checks are carried out by the Dental Estimates Board which approves fees for certain procedures and institutes random checks on the quality of work performed. This system can never exclude the possibility of unnecessary work. It has, for example, been suggested that a proportion of tooth cavities caused by caries would remineralize without treatment. But, in a fee-for-service system the incentive is for the dentist to drill out and fill the cavity rather than to wait. Indeed, it is impossible to check on a wholly unscrupulous dentist who 'fills' a non-existent cavity and claims payment for doing so.

The other main problem with fee-for-service is that it can distort the definition of health need and health care by reducing health to procedures which can be itemized for payment. For certain parts of medical practice this may be convenient, but for many patient's health problems, defining health widely (see Chapter 9), it tends to be inappropriate. Empathy, understanding and long-term emotional support, for example, are difficult to itemize and indeed, were they to be so, their nature might well be changed: 'friendship-for-a-fee' is very different from friendship.

Capitation

Capitation is a system in which the doctor is paid according to how many patients he or she looks after, irrespective of whether they use the service. Thus two doctors with the same number of patients on their lists – and hence the same income – might work significantly different hours if one group of patients uses the service more than the other.

This system, in effect, works like the old Chinese method of paying the doctor whereby the doctor was paid by patients when they were healthy and not paid when they were ill. The doctor therefore receives a higher income, relative to the work performed, the healthier the patient population. The key advantage of this system is that the doctor (as well as the patient) profits from good health, whereas under fee-for-service the doctor benefits from ill health. Emphasis is therefore, in principle, placed on preventive measures, on support services and long-term care, etc. in an effort to improve the general health of the population served. (In contrast prevention under a fee-for-service system is in a somewhat ambivalent position because though it might gain an immediate fee it potentially reduces future earnings.)

One of the main problems with a system which works by encouraging current effort to improve patients' health, is that such a strategy might not decrease future workload. There is not sufficient evidence to support the belief that hard work by the doctor today will improve patients' health such that they consult less frequently in the future. Indeed it has even been argued that the opposite effect holds: over-concern with patients and their problems merely makes them more dependent and even more likely to consult in future (see Chapter 13).

The other problem with capitation is that instead of being concerned with patients' health over time, the doctor may come to be more concerned with how often they use the services offered today. In other words, low consultation rates instead of being used as indicators of good health become ends in themselves. The result is that if the doctor wishes to increase income relative to work input, there is an incentive to undertake the health care of too many patients and to give them only summary attention when they seek help.

A large component of the pay of the British general practitioner is based on capitation. This means that they have lists of patients for whom they have taken responsibility to provide care. The general practitioner is therefore in a position to provide continuity of care to this relatively fixed and well defined population. This has not prevented the introduction of other techniques, based on both the stick and the carrot, further to encourage general practitioners to provide good quality services.

Salary

The salary is, as it suggests, a fixed income irrespective of the work performed. It has the same advantages as capitation in that it acts as a disincentive to over-zealous and unnecessary investigation and treatment. Moreover it has an advantage over the capitation system in that there is no incentive to take on more patients than can reasonably be managed (though 'excess' patients might then find themselves on waiting lists and in queues). However, it also has the same disadvantage in that there is no incentive to work hard. Even if there are fixed hours the doctor has no financial encouragement to work quickly and efficiently within them.

Overview

When comparing systems of paying the doctor it is as well to remember that, despite its undoubted appeal, money is not the only incentive behind good clinical practice. In the same way that the excesses of a fee-for-service system might be tempered by professional commitment to good medicine, so the disincentives in the capitation and salaried systems are often overcome by doctors' pride and satisfaction in providing good medical care. The method of payment therefore, rather than dictating practice, tends to distort its emphasis, in particular how health need is defined and met by medical practitioners.

In any health care system it is not unusual to find a mixture of methods of payment which illustrate the deficiencies of one or the other. Thus public health doctors are usually salaried even in an otherwise fee-for-service system and doctors paid by salary or capitation are often offered fees for specific services when these are deemed important enough to need encouraging, e.g. immunization, contraception.

Otherwise the chief disadvantages with salary and capitation as methods of payment have to be contrasted with those of fee-for-service. To a certain extent it might be argued that the tendency of capitation and salaried personnel to under-treat may be a more acceptable error than over-treatment, especially in view of the problems of effectiveness and efficiency of modern medicine (see Chapter 13). The other significant advantage of salary and capitation over fee-for-service is the relative cheapness of the former, both in terms of direct payments to doctors (medical profession tend to do better from the latter), and in terms of the additional costs incurred by doctors' clinical decisions. This acts as an incentive for governments to adopt the cheaper system; and its greater ability to encompass a wider definition of health, e.g. to include psychosocial factors, probably make it potentially more able to meet total health needs.

● **Evaluating doctors' decisions**

The methods of constraining clinical autonomy outlined above involve trying to control various input factors in clinical decision-making. The alternative is to persuade doctors directly to monitor their own work or to introduce more third party evaluation of the results of those decisions.

Clinical audit

Increasingly doctors are being persuaded to introduce their own 'quality control' in clinical practice. This can take various forms but essentially depends on the doctors measuring important aspects of their work, especially outcomes of intervention, on a regular basis to determine the maintenance of standards. Any slippage needs to be identified and appropriate corrective action taken.

So long as doctors are willing to review the quality of their own work, then the more likely they are to be able to keep the clinical autonomy that they so value; the alternative is to accept assessment by third parties.

Peer review

One means of preserving the principle of medical autonomy yet assessing an individual doctor's work is to introduce a peer review mechanism. In the USA, because of the dangers of over-operating as a result of the fee-for-service system, many hospitals have peer review committees to examine the pathology reports on surgically-removed organs. If surgeons are over-operating then more histologically normal tissues are likely to be removed. This enables such surgeons to be identified and brought to task.

The UK has fewer peer review procedures, partly because over-treatment is not such a problem (except, perhaps, in the fee-for-service world of general dental practice). However, there is one form of peer review which deserves separate mention, and that is the Confidential Enquiry into Maternal Mortality.

In the 1950s a Confidential Enquiry was set up to examine the circumstances surrounding any woman's death during pregnancy and childbirth. The Enquiry team is composed largely of professional members, and is required to take evidence from all concerned, reach a conclusion as to whether the death was preventable, and if so, who was to be held responsible.

Because the Enquiry works confidentially it is not a direct threat to clinical autonomy – even doctors who are held responsible for a woman's death in some way are not named. People are therefore happy to give evidence in the knowledge that the conclusions of the study might help tighten up procedures such that there would be no recurrence. In the event, maternal mortality has dropped sharply since the inception of the Enquiry, and though it is impossible to say whether the latter has been responsible, it may well have played a part.

Performance indicators

In recent years management philosophy has moved towards performance indicators and performance-related pay. Choosing suitable indicators for clinical practice would be difficult, but probably could be done for some types of routine work. In some ways DRGs are a weak form of performance indicator; the idea is likely to spread in years to come so long as health services are struggling to gain maximum benefit for money spent.

Patient assessments

Other than doctors and managers, the other group which is in a position to comment on clinical decisions is patients.

Satisfaction and complaints

To allow some redress against bad or inappropriate medical decisions various complaints procedures have emerged. Some medical decisions are so mistaken that they go to litigation, but many are relatively minor and only require that the doctor has some negative feedback to take into account for the next time a similar situation presents itself.

In the USA these problems are not so important. Patients there go to litigation with more enthusiasm and besides, in a basically private system, consumers can vote with their feet. In the UK, with a long tradition of deference to medical authority, it has proved difficult to establish a fair and effective complaints machinery: very often it is hampered by constraints on the type of complaint which can be made, the time span after the incident in which it can be reported, the over-representation of doctors themselves on the adjudication panel, and the triviality of many penalties.

There are two alternative strategies: one is to encourage more 'consumerism' in which patients are encouraged to change doctors, get second opinions, or go outside the NHS if they do not get satisfaction. The other is to encourage health authorities to monitor patient satisfaction directly by means of surveys (DHSS, 1987).

Professional discipline

The medical profession has been given control over the content of its own work but part of that 'contract' with society is that it will police its own members and discipline them as necessary. In the USA this is the responsibility of the State medical disciplinary boards. They are dominated by the medical profession, and have proved reluctant to discipline doctors for clinical incompetence other than that brought about by illness or frank criminal behaviour. The result is that Americans have turned to the law courts to obtain redress.

In the UK, the responsibility for disciplining doctors has also been controlled by doctors themselves, in this case through the General Medical Council. Again, the GMC has claimed difficulty in evaluating clinical competence directly, and has tended to concentrate on the five 'A's of alcoholism, advertising, addiction, adultery and abortion (though since the legalization of abortion, the latter less so). This has led to a greater willingness to seek legal recompense (as evidenced by the rapidly increasing medical insurance premiums payable by doctors), though not to the extent of the USA for reasons mentioned below. There is, in addition, a growing pressure on the GMC to address the issue of clinical competence in a more robust fashion (Rosenthal, 1987). In the absence of proper professional self-regulation, it can be expected that call for government intervention will increase, as will the tide of cases entering the legal system.

Litigation

If all else fails, and the problem is sufficiently serious, patients have the right to pursue the medical profession in court for redress. In practice this is a very common strategy in the USA, but relatively rare in the UK.

First, it is probably fair to say that Americans are more litigious, being more prepared to use the law courts to obtain redress (and usually massive settlements if successful).

Second, American lawyers are allowed to use the 'contingency fee' system in which they are paid only if successful. This means that there is no financial risk for patients to go to court, and there is usually a generous percentage of any settlement for the winning lawyer. This has led to some lawyers deliberately seeking out dissatisfied patients to try and win a large sum in court. To pay for this system, medical insurance is very high – for some high risk specialties several tens of thousands of dollars annually – and this tends either to dissuade doctors from entering certain specialties or to result in high fees.

American court settlements can be extraordinarily high and there is continuing doubt as to whether the increasing costs can be carried by doctors and hospitals. One solution being mooted is to separate compensation from the issue of whether the doctor has been negligent by setting up a no-fault insurance plan which would compensate patients whatever the cause of their problem (Rosenthal, 1987); this would still leave a need for a strengthened medical disciplinary procedure to identify and deal with those incompetent doctors whose actions can be so harmful to their patients.

● **References**

Abel-Smith, B. (1976) *Value for Money in Health Services,* Heinemann, London

DHSS (1976) *Sharing Resources for Health in England: Report of the Resource Allocation Working Party,* HMSO, London

DHSS (1987) *Promoting Better Health: The Government's Programme for Improving Primary Health Care,* HMSO, London

Freidson, E. (1970) *Profession of Medicine,* Dodd Mead, New York

Goode, W. J. (1960) Encroachment, charlatanism and the emerging profession: psychiatry, sociology and medicine. *American Sociological Review,* **25**, 902–914

Johnson, T. J. (1972) *Professions and Power,* Macmillan, London

Rosenthal, M. (1987) *Dealing With Medical Malpractice: The British and Swedish Experience,* Tavistock, London

12

Delivering health care

Although some health care is provided by all countries there are a variety of ways by which it is delivered. These range from a market system in which health care is treated as any other private commodity, to that of provision by government on the basis of need, with various forms of health insurance in between. The particular choice of system found in a country reflects both its history and its current political philosophy, the market system being more likely to be supported by the political right and government provision by the left. Although no Western country has an exclusive market or State system of delivering health care, examination of their key features and differences can illuminate some crucial issues in understanding health care delivery.

● Allocating scarce resources

Health care, as any economic system of production and distribution, starts with the assumption of scarce resources. There are not enough goods – in this case health services – to enable everyone to consume what they would like. It follows that there needs to be a mechanism for distributing these scarce resources in some way.

The market system

The solution of the market economy to the problem of scarce resources is to allow individual consumers to make choices about how they will spend their incomes. As incomes are limited, consumers must choose between alternatives: buying a car, perhaps, or a holiday, or a surgical operation. Taken together these different consumer choices focus attention on shortages in the economy: whether people wish to buy cars, holidays or operations will determine where future expansion in production will lie. Thus if there is greater demand for cars than operations, productive resources will move from surgery into car production. The mechanism for this movement is the 'profit motive' as producers see there is more money to be made from producing cars than carrying out operations. In addition, because of the demand for cars it would be expected that the salaries available in the car industry would be greater than those available in surgery, in which case people would change jobs and gradually move into those parts of the economy which were expanding to meet consumer demand.

In practice, of course, major shifts in salaries do not occur as there are various mechanisms in Western societies which prevent such radical changes; these are customs which, economists say, make the market 'inefficient'. Nevertheless, the central feature of the market economy, namely consumer choice and efficient shifts in production in response to that choice, remain essential features of the market economy.

The command system

The other way of organizing the production and distribution of resources in an economy is the command or directed economy. In this system people's needs are determined by central authorities. In other words it is not what the consumer wishes or demands which affects what they consume, but rather what they need. Once all needs have been determined then production is organized to meet those needs and income is allocated to people to enable them to buy the needs which have been determined for them.

This system can go hopelessly wrong and can be remarkably inefficient. Traditional East European economies are renowned for deciding that their populations will need so many pairs of shoes per year, producing these shoes, then finding that the population chooses not to buy them. However the principle is an important one: that the function of an economic system is to meet people's needs rather than their more capricious wishes, which are themselves dependent on having the resources to satisfy them.

Striking a balance

Insofar as delivering health care is concerned a market economy treats health care as a commodity. This means that while people have a choice – whether to buy it or not – some people will find that they do not have the resources to buy the amount they feel they need. The command economy, on the other hand, treats health care as a right of all citizens. In this case State provision ensures equity, that is to each according to his or her health needs. Table 12.1 shows some of these differences.

Health care provision in all countries seems to be constantly in a state of flux. No country seems to get it perfectly 'right'. The reason for this is that an ideal health care system would probably take the idea of choice together with the efficiency of resource allocation from the market system, and the meeting of all

Table 12.1 Differences between market and State provision of health care

	Market	State provision
Health care	A commodity	A right
Consumer options	Wishes choice	Needs no choice
Resource allocation	'Invisible hand' efficient	Explicit rationing 'inefficient'
Access	Unequal	Equity
Social justice	Unfair to many	Fair

health needs from the command system. The paradox is that as choice/efficiency are increased so the level of equity usually declines, and vice versa. This pattern can be seen if we look at the changes in health care provision over the last few decades in the USA and UK.

● The market for health care in the USA

The political principle underpinning the US health care system is the market place. This means that citizens, in theory, are not dictated to by government but have free choice in their decisions about what health services to consume. In addition, taken together, these choices direct and redirect health resources to ensure an efficient system of allocating facilities. However, as has been pointed out earlier, such a system produces a problem for those people who do not have the resources to gain access to the market place. Moreover, even for those people who do have resources, health is an unpredictable state, meaning that large expenses can accrue quickly and unexpectedly. Thus, whereas expenditure on items such as transport, housing, food, etc. can be fairly reliably predicted and therefore allowed for, health expenditure for an individual can be almost non-existent one year, then sudden and large the next.

The usual strategy for dealing with unpredictable and costly risks is insurance. Few people are willing to risk the cost of rebuilding their house after a major fire or replacing their car after a major accident: they therefore take out insurance. This means, in effect, that all people taking out insurance spread the cost of replacing the relatively few damaged cars or houses when they occur. Exactly the same principle applies to health care. All the people who take out insurance spread the risk and therefore the cost of paying for expensive medical bills.

In the United States there have been two ways in which the insurance principle has been used to control health risks. First, insurance can be taken out indirectly with a third party, either an insurance company or the State, which will guarantee to arrange whatever services have been contracted for. Secondly, insurance can be taken out directly with the health providers, either doctors or hospitals.

Third party insurance

The commonest way for Americans to pay for their health care is to take out insurance with a third party insurance company. This can be done privately or through an employer's scheme with the employer paying or contributing to the premiums. However, because there are people who do not have resources to take out adequate insurance, there is a risk that some ill people could be denied access to any health care at all. This has been seen as politically and socially unacceptable – even though the market system would argue that some people should go without health care, just as some people go without a car – so the government, in recent years, has intervened to provide insurance cover for those who lack the financial means to provide it themselves. The well-known schemes are Medicare for old people and Medicaid for the very poor. In a sense these schemes represent a sort of compulsory, subsidized insurance through government.

The insurer, either private company or government, agrees to meet the costs of health care needed by the consumer. The consumer then visits doctors or hospitals, is charged a fee for the services rendered and then either the consumer, or the doctor, reclaims the money from the insurance body.

While the insurance principle enables the consumer to deal with the unexpected and high cost of health care, the principle does undermine the central market discipline that consumers have limited resources and therefore must choose between competing demands. This problem is magnified by a key difference between health care demands and claims made under other insurance policies such as for a car or house. In the latter there is both an upper limit on the claim – presumably the cost of replacement – and a general agreement of what counts as a legitimate claim. In health care however, especially with new and expensive treatments, there might be no clear 'maximum' claim and little agreement on what is really needed in a particular case. In effect, having taken out insurance, consumers are able to consume health services with few real constraints. The net effect of this situation has been steeply rising costs of health care in the USA both for private insurance companies and for government.

In an attempt to bring this situation under some sort of control in recent years, insurers and government have been trying to limit costs. Three strategies have been tried:

1. One approach is to shift some of the costs back on to the consumer to act as a disincentive to further use. Thus patients might be required to pay for certain specific services or a percentage of the cost of others. Faced with such costs consumers might be persuaded to limit their demands; however this strategy is only of limited scope as the whole principle of insurance is to remove the threat of significant immediate direct costs.
2. Another approach is to meet the consumers' health needs but to limit choice to certain cost-contained health services. One scheme which has increased in popularity in recent years is the Preferred Provider Organization (PPO). A Preferred Provider Organization involves the insurer in negotiating a discount on the usual fees with either hospitals or doctors. Patients with insurance are then informed that they can only obtain medical care from these designated providers.
3. The other strategy is to limit the amount of payment to doctors and hospitals on the basis of the patient's particular medical problem. These diagnosis-related groups, or DRGs (see previous chapter), encourage both doctor and hospital to restrain their expenditure to the expected amount they will receive.

Problems with third party insurance

The problem with relying on private third party insurance as a solution for a nation's health care is that it fails to cover large groups of the population. In the USA this has meant the government intervening to provide care for those groups who have been missed. Even so, there are still large sections of the American population who do not have any insurance cover nor are they poor enough to be covered by the government safety net. In addition, many people who take out insurance only buy a limited policy which may not provide sufficient cover for the expenses of a catastrophic illness. The net effect of this is that patients faced with large medical bills first use their insurance cover to pay them, as far as it will go; next they pay with their own money – this may involve them selling all their material assets; then, when they are virtually destitute, they will qualify for government support through Medicaid. For this reason the largest cause of individual bankruptcy in the USA is health care costs. (In practice some of these bankruptcies are only technical in that some people arrange their financial affairs so as to appear poor enough to qualify for Medicaid when large medical bills are seen as imminent.)

A second problem of third party insurance cover is the inefficiency and bureaucratic costs involved. There are many insurance companies and an individual patient may have several policies; health care providers (doctors and hospitals) need to provide a bill for every service they render, and send this to the appropriate insuring body. This means that every procedure carried out on a patient (drugs, investigations, operations, etc.) needs to be separately billed and the bill assigned to a relevant insurance body. American hospitals therefore have large departments entirely concerned with this billing procedure, moving large amounts of paper around the different suppliers and consumers. This massive bureaucratic waste is particularly ironic in view of the supposed efficiency of the pure market system.

The third range of problems which third party insurance meets concerns the strategies that providers use to get round insurers' attempts at cost-containment (such as the constraints of DRGs described in the preceding chapter), which further limit consumer choice and add to the inefficiency of the system.

Pre-paid health plans

The other way of using insurance to cover the risks and costs of ill health is through an insurance arrangement whereby premiums are paid directly to the health care providers rather than being routed through a third party insurance company. The commonest type of such a scheme is the Health Maintenance Organization (HMO). An HMO employs its own doctors, usually on a salary, and either owns local hospitals or enters a contract with them to cover so much use per annum. Consumers register at annual intervals with an HMO and make regular monthly payments, and for this the HMO agrees to cover all their health needs during the relevant year.

A variant of an HMO is the Independent Practice Association (IPA). Again an annual contract is taken out with the IPA which consists of an association of doctors who have agreed to operate in this way. (They are otherwise fee-for-service doctors in the market system.) In meeting the patient's health needs over the year the doctor may overspend the IPA fee in which case a loss is made; on the other hand underspending produces a profit which is shared between the IPA and doctor.

The financial success of HMOs can be gauged by the fact that they turn out to be 10–40% cheaper than traditional fee-for-service medical practice. Their success seems to be mainly in keeping patients out of hospital which is the most expensive part of health care. In addition, in having mainly salaried doctors there is no incentive for doctors to overtreat. Doctors employed by HMOs also undergo very close audit of their work patterns and workload.

Problems of pre-paid health plans
It has been said that the salaried doctors who are attracted to HMOs are those doctors who are unable to make a living in the usual fee-for-service

environment. Critics of HMOs, therefore, often argue that HMO doctors tend to be clinically less able – or, more charitably, it might be that they are less business-like. The suspicion that they are less competent, coupled with the fact that their salaried status leads them to undertreat rather than overtreat, has led to a belief in the USA that the quality of care given by HMOs is less than that given by traditional fee-for-service medicine.

Secondly, just as hospitals who are operating DRGs may carefully select the sorts of patients they treat, so HMOs have a financial incentive only to treat patients who by and large are healthy. Elderly patients, patients with chronic illness, etc. may therefore find it difficult to join an HMO.

The third practical difficulty of HMOs is arranging health cover when patients are outside the area. A patient taken ill on holiday or requiring urgent accident and emergency treatment can reclaim the costs from their HMO but only within very strict guidelines.

Summary of market system

The main advantages of the market system are the choice it gives the consumer and the efficiency with which it allocates resources between different parts of the health care sector. Its major problem however is that of access for those who cannot afford to enter the market. In other words, the fact that equity – the provision of services on the basis of need – is not a central feature of the market must be addressed by compensatory actions by individuals and governments. The resulting strategy of using insurance, via third party insurance company, government funded health care, or HMOs, does meet many of the problems of access, but in their train they bring further problems.

1. They compromise the choice which the market system is meant to give. Patients with insurance or in HMOs are severely constrained in the amount of 'shopping around' they are permitted to carry out.
2. The efficiency of the system is weakened. Insurance and fee-for-service leads to large bureaucracies. In addition the allocation of health care resources is distorted artificially by the assumptions used to create restraints such as diagnosis-related groups.

It does seem ironic that in coping with the weaknesses of the market system, the major advantages of the market are lost and the sorts of problems which are said to bedevil direct government provision of health care are regularly faced. This does not mean that the market system, as a political principle, is seriously weakened. Indeed there are regular moves to improve the operation of the health care market in the USA. For example, the monopoly position of health care providers, particularly doctors, is a serious impediment to the market and successive US governments have tried to oppose such monopolies by encouraging advertising, liberalizing entry into medicine, etc. In addition patients' position in the market has been strengthened by improving patient knowledge (the idea of fully informed consent) and by enabling litigation to proceed when consumers are dissatisfied.

● **Government provision of health care in the UK**
The political philosophy behind health care provision in the UK starts from a very different point from that in the USA. In the UK the guiding principle is

equity, that is the provision of health care on the basis of need. Health care should not therefore be given to someone because they either have high status, power or wealth, but because they need the care. In the main doctors are paid by salary and capitation so they have no incentive to assign health services other than on the basis of need. In addition resources are allocated supposedly solely on the basis of patient needs.

Problems of State health care provision

1. The major problem with a principle of equity is that someone needs to define need. Who should do this? Doctors? Politicians? Managers?
2. A related problem is the need to ration services in an explicit way. In the market system services are rationed by the ability of people to pay. Because no payment is made in a wholly government-provided system, which is free at the point of delivery, there have to be other rationing mechanisms which may be politically unpopular.
3. Thirdly, because health need is defined by people other than the patient, the system tends to be paternalistic and takes little heed of consumer choice.
4. Finally the system is said to be inefficient in the way it allocates resources because it is unresponsive to rapid changes in health care needs.

Improving choice and efficiency

Some of the above problems have been dealt with by permitting, and in recent years encouraging, a private sector for health care delivery. This enables patients to have choice within the private sector and choice between the private and public (with the proviso, of course, that only those with resources are able to make these choices). For a government-provided health care system such as the NHS other strategies have been used to cope with the above problems.

First there have been constant attempts to improve administrative coherence and management efficiency. This has been tackled by either reorganizing the administrative structure of the health service or, especially in recent years, by introducing professional managers into health care delivery to ensure efficient use of resources.

Secondly, clinical autonomy, which has traditionally enabled doctors to define need and dispense resources, has been constrained in recent years by government intervention. Doctors have been restricted to a limited list for drug prescribing; hospital consultants have often been given specific budgets for their activities; doctors have been informed of the costs of the various procedures they carry out.

Thirdly, the government has intervened to try and make resource allocation as rational as possible. The major strategy here has been the Resource Allocation Working Party (RAWP). Using the RAWP formula funds have been allocated to different regions of the health service on the basis of their population and health care need as measured by mortality figures. This has meant a relatively large redistribution of resources between the north and south of the country.

These various strategies have, arguably, made the health care system more efficient. However market economists argue that efficiency is only achieved and maintained in a healthy, competitive environment. It thus appears that more competition in the health service will become common. This can already be seen in the privatization of various facets of the health service such as catering and laundry facilities. It can also be seen in government proposals to make general practitioners more competitive for their patients, and in proposals to have internal markets in which various services can be traded between different geographical health authorities.

As well as improving efficiency a competitive environment should also improve the service to consumers. Again, the government seems intent on improving consumer choice.

Summary of direct government provision

From starting with the principle of equity the government-funded NHS in the UK has gradually moved towards some of the features of the US system. Efficiency through competitiveness and wider consumer choice, it is believed, can help improve the NHS. However as suggested earlier, the extension of the market principles of competition and choice threaten to undermine the underlying principle of the NHS which is equity. Thus the most efficient health care system may override or ignore the health care needs of some people: and the wider the choice given to consumers the more likely it is that some consumers, but not others, are in a position to choose better health care. As in the USA, attempts to compensate for the inherent weaknesses and disadvantages of the particular health care delivery system tend to compromise the underlying principle.

● **Towards a National Health Service**
A brief overview of the history of health care in the UK illustrates many of the issues discussed above.

Late nineteenth century

In the late nineteenth century five different forms of health care delivery can be identified.

1. Poor law institutions, funded by local communities, had existed for several centuries to provide a safety net for those who were too poor or destitute to look after themselves. Because of the close link between poverty and illness, poor law institutions towards the end of the nineteenth century were increasingly filled with chronically ill people. They were thus coming to act as hospitals.
2. During the early part of the nineteenth century philanthropists had founded voluntary, private hospitals. These operated on the basis of private subscriptions to provide free care for poor people. These hospitals tended only to treat acute illnesses rather than chronic.
3. During the middle of the nineteenth century the public health movement in the UK had removed many environmental causes of illness. Through sanitation, hygiene, improved nutrition, etc. the health of the population, in urban areas in particular, had been considerably improved. Public health doctors who monitored the environmental hazards were employed by local governments.

4. In the late nineteenth century groups of workers had collected together to form Friendly Societies through which to arrange health insurance. In effect these were rather like HMOs. Members of the Society paid a regular premium and the Society engaged the services of doctors, on a capitation basis, to look after its members.
5. Private practice was the usual health care system for middle class people. Patients consulted doctors giving a fee for the service.

Early twentieth century

Public health and private practice continued into the twentieth century little changed, as did the voluntary hospitals. The old Poor Law workhouses, however, became more recognizable as hospitals, albeit with a bias towards caring for the chronically ill. Control of these passed formally to local government.

The major change in the early twentieth century was in the field of primary health care. In 1911 with the first major piece of health care legislation the government introduced National Health Insurance (NHI) to replace and extend the locally-based Friendly Societies. Like the Friendly Societies, NHI mainly covered low income employees for primary health care services, doctors being still employed on a capitation basis.

By the late inter-war years the health care system was showing some signs of strain. Five particular problems can be identified: each of these problems has their parallel in recent US history.

1. There was considerable regional variation. Patients in one part of the country (paying the same National Health Insurance premium) were receiving very different levels of service compared with patients in another.
2. The system was administratively inefficient. National Health Insurance had simply maintained the local committee structure of the Friendly Societies, and these were bureaucratic and slow.
3. There were poor clinical conditions in primary health care. Remuneration through National Health Insurance was poor, nor was there any incentive for general practitioners to improve their clinical conditions and surgeries.
4. By the Second World War the charitable voluntary hospitals were finding themselves in difficult financial circumstances. The regularly increasing costs of acute medicine exceeded their limited subscription income, and in an attempt to bolster the state of voluntary hospitals the government had provided direct funding. The net effect of this was that by the Second World War about half of voluntary hospital funds were coming directly from central government.
5. The people who, arguably, had the worst health care provision in the inter-war years were the middle classes. Working class patients were covered for general practitioner care by NHI, and their hospital care was provided for free either by local government hospitals or by the voluntary hospitals. Middle class patients however did not, in the main, benefit from these various schemes and had to pay the usual fee-for-service. The more well-off middle class patients could manage these expenses. However lower middle class patients found that doctors' bills were, as in the USA today, financially ruinous.

The National Health Service (NHS)

During the Second World War many of these problems were overcome when the government introduced an emergency medical service. After the war the benefits of such a service were apparent, and the government resolved to bring in a national system of health care. This system would also address many of the problems identified above.

Although the NHS is often presented as a major piece of health legislation, its introduction in 1948 simply involved some reorganization and extension of existing schemes.

1. Public health, which since the mid nineteenth century had been carried out from a local government base, continued unchanged.
2. Hospitals which had either been funded by local government or, in the case of voluntary hospitals, largely by central government, were wholly taken over by the Ministry of Health. This created an integrated hospital system. MOH
3. National Health Insurance which had provided primary health care services to low paid employees was extended to the whole population. Thus the principle of health care free at the point of delivery was extended to the whole population.

Future of the NHS

Over the succeeding years various adjustments have been made to the NHS, but its essential form has remained essentially unchanged. Local government has virtually lost all control of health care provision as the service has been centralized (though a debate continues as to whether local control might solve many problems). There have been various boundary changes between NHS geographical areas, as the most efficient organization of services has been pursued; in related moves more professional management structures and procedures have been introduced, many with the aim of containing doctors' expenditure.

There was a belief in 1948 that the NHS would decrease the amount of illness in the community so that its costs would decline. This was very much mistaken: costs have risen over three-fold in real terms (that is allowing for inflation). The NHS is a major cost to central government (though considerably less in terms of GNP than other Western countries) and many recent changes have been taken with the goal of increasing value for money.

Politically, in recent years, the theme of consumer choice has been important: it has been argued that consumers should be able to choose, and their choices will increase competition so that the quality of care will improve. While not disagreeing with these goals, critics have pointed out that some of the policies introduced to achieve them threaten the very existence of the NHS and its credo of health care, free at the point of delivery, to those in need. However, major change seems unlikely. By international standards the NHS is cheap, relatively efficient and well distributed. Certainly to many, especially those working in it, it is in a state of crisis, but arguably it has been in this state for several decades and still survived: perhaps one of its fundamental characteristics is this constant plight, while alternatives are debated, and then rejected as offering less than the current system. Moreover, at the moment, it has sufficient public backing to ensure that its principles and fundamental structure remain intact.

13

Evaluating health care

What is the value of a health care system? What are its costs and benefits, its advantages and disadvantages? Four different questions can be asked of a particular health service:

1. Is it effective/efficient?
2. Does it meet 'real' needs?
3. Is it fair?
4. Is it iatrogenic?

● Is the health care system effective/efficient?

It is obvious that health services should be effective, otherwise they are a waste of time and resources. In addition, given that all health care systems work with scarce resources, it is important that health care is efficient. Efficiency means that maximum benefit is obtained for each unit of resources. Two drugs might be equally effective at treating a patient, but if one costs twice as much as the other, then the more efficient treatment is the cheaper one.

A health problem has its own natural history such that at some point there is an outcome. Thus:

$$\text{health problem} \xrightarrow{\text{natural history}} \text{outcome N.}$$

The goal of a health service is to intervene in the natural history of the problem using certain resources or inputs to produce a more desirable outcome. Thus:

$$\text{health problem} \xrightarrow{} \text{outcome D.}$$
input

Each of these terms can be variously defined and measured.

Health problems

Health problems may be of a whole population, a small group or an individual. Some of the range of ways of defining and measuring health problems has been described in Chapter 3.

Inputs

Again inputs can range in extent, depending on the problem being addressed, from the percentage of Gross National Product devoted to health services, to a particular drug or procedure. For evaluation purposes, inputs are often reduced to their financial cost, thereby establishing a common currency for comparisons. For some aspects of health care, especially those relating to emotional and social support, the reduction to monetary costs is both difficult and, arguably, inappropriate.

Outcomes

The outcome measures used to assess the benefits of health care intervention are much the same as those used to measure health problems in the first place. Indeed the treatment of one health problem may produce, as an outcome, another health problem. If intervention has been successful, the latter should be some improvement over the former.

One of the commonest measures of outcome for health services has been infant mortality. Infant mortality figures are often used in international comparisons, and to examine the progress of health services on a year by year basis. However, given the evidence of the influence of social factors on mortality, it is probable that medical intervention plays a very small part in the overall figures. Otherwise, it is very difficult to measure the overall effectiveness of health care systems. If it were easy, there would be less debate about the most appropriate form of its organization (see Chapter 12).

Randomized controlled clinical trials

To evaluate the effectiveness of a particular input or intervention, it is necessary to compare the initial state with the result or outcome. But an improvement does not necessarily imply that the intervention was effective. This is because the natural course of the health problem may have produced exactly the same outcome without the intervention having any influence. For example, if the common cold were to be treated with antibiotics, it would be found that all patients were cured. But the reason they were cured was not the antibiotics but the natural course of the disease.

In any evaluation it is therefore important to allow for other influences, particularly natural progression, on the outcome. The way round this problem was discovered several decades ago when the randomized controlled clinical trial came into use. Patients, for whom a certain treatment may be of benefit, are randomly allocated to an experimental and a control group. The point about randomization is that, if carried out successfully, it distributes all other factors, known and unknown, which might affect outcome evenly between both groups so that any difference in outcome must be due to the intervention.

The experimental group receives the treatment (preferably 'blind') and the control group receives a placebo, and the outcome of the two groups is then compared. If the outcome in the experimental group is better than the outcome in the control group then it can be said that the treatment is effective; on the other hand, if outcomes are similar in both groups then the treatment is ineffective.

It has been argued that with these techniques the use of various treatment regimes in medicine can be objectively evaluated (Cochrane, 1972). Nevertheless, it has been estimated that less than 20% of all medical interventions have been properly evaluated for their effectiveness. Medicine continues to rely on 'tried and tested' interventions which have not been shown to be effective nor, and in some ways more important, shown to be safe. Arguably a lot more can be done to test and improve the effectiveness and efficiency of medical intervention. Such a policy, however, would require the close cooperation and involvement of the medical profession. Chapter 11 has already outlined some of the difficulties in involving doctors in policies which may constrain their clinical autonomy.

Comparing benefits

Even accepting that one treatment is better than another, does this justify its use on a patient who would benefit from it? The answer may seem clear. Yet, given that the resources of a health service are finite, by providing one patient with an effective therapy for a problem another patient is deprived of those same resources. If renal dialysis is provided for a patient, the cost of that treatment is not then available to provide care for a geriatric patient, or an improved antenatal service, or radiotherapy for a cancer. All health systems, whether implicitly or explicitly, are involved in some sort of rationing (Aaron and Schwartz, 1984).

In these terms the doctor's action in helping one patient is, paradoxically, depriving another patient. Thus, although doctors are taught to treat individual patients to the best of their ability, and though they may be wise enough only to use effective methods, doctors are in fact constantly making non-individual judgements, as their decision to treat one patient is also a decision to allocate resources away from other potential patients the doctor probably has not even seen or may not know about. Every treatment is in effect a judgement on priorities which involves deciding what the health service is trying to do, in particular how it is defining the health needs it sets out to meet.

- **Does the health care system meet the 'real' needs of its consumers?**

Health services

Before it is possible to decide whether a health service is meeting its goals – presumably to meet the health needs of its population – there must be some agreement as to what are the appropriate aims. To many people a legitimate goal of health services might be to save lives. But the evidence presented in Chapter 4 would suggest that, over the years, medicine has not been very successful at this task. Indeed while therapeutic value might be the chief rationale for a health service, it is clear from the problems of measurement (see Chapter 4) that these are difficult to quantify as many factors other than the existence of a health service seem to affect therapeutic outcomes. Indeed, using the arguments advanced in Chapter 4 on the influence of social factors on morbidity and mortality, it might be argued that the specific therapeutic effect of a health service is probably fairly low in terms of lives saved or people cured – housing or diet for example probably have greater influence.

Yet to evaluate medicine by mortality would be needlessly to restrict it to a narrow range of operation. Indeed, the failure of medicine to make a marked impression on mortality led McKeown (1979) to argue that the role of medicine was wider than increasing life expectancy. He suggested that medicine had four important roles: 'To assist us to come safely into the world and comfortably out of it, and during life to protect the well and care for the sick and disabled.' Though these goals may be less glamorous than those of curative medicine they may be no less socially desirable. And while they too present considerable measurement problems ('What is good care?') it is apparent that in the context of the huge demands on health services for health care they probably represent important outcome criteria of effectiveness.

Specific treatments

What is the appropriate goal of specific treatments? This might be clear if a treatment has an obvious benefit to health, but often different treatments have different advantages. When two drugs are being compared in a randomized controlled clinical trial, it might be found that drug A is better than drug B because it saves more lives or that drug C is better than drug D because it relieves more pain. Both these outcome criteria are selections from a potentially long list, e.g. death, comfort, happiness, ability to work, normal blood count, etc. and they represent selections from different criteria over time.

Thus, although drug A might save more lives than drug B over a 5-year period, drug B might also enable more people to go back to work. Although drug C may relieve more pain than drug D, the latter may improve the long-term prognosis. Many of these variations in outcome are known: certain drugs reduce hypertension but produce impotence, certain drugs relieve epilepsy but damage the fetus, etc. Yet compared with the outcomes – good and bad – that are known, most outcomes are unknown, either because they have not been thought important enough to measure or they are too difficult to measure. Coronary care units may be no more effective in terms of mortality than home care for myocardial infarction, but what of patient contentment, family relations, anxiety, social cost, etc? If these criteria were used coronary care units might be found to be more (or less) effective than care at home.

This is not only to argue for the importance of extending outcome criteria to include more psychosocial variables, but to point to inherent constraints in evaluating two therapies. All the effects of medical intervention can never be known, but the types of effects that are chosen to be examined will, in certain ways, bias the sort of health care provided. If, for example, outcome measures are restricted to mortality, a health service will be created which emphasizes extended life at the expense of other important aspects of people's lives.

●   **Is the health care system fair?**

The fairness of health care would not be universally agreed as a valid criterion by which a health service should be analysed. Nevertheless, particularly for those health services in which health care is viewed as a right, and not as a tradeable commodity, the idea of social justice is very important. If all citizens have an equal entitlement to health care, then this provides a criterion by which a health service can be evaluated.

Insofar as the British NHS is concerned, the issue of fairness has been hotly debated, especially with regard to equality of access. There tends to be an assumption that once a patient reaches the doctor, his problem will be dealt with on a clinical basis, and no fear or favour will be shown to particular patients because of their background or status. But there probably has been inequality in getting access to health care in the first place. Three forms of inequality have been identified.

Geographical inequalities

The NHS came into being in 1948 by simply taking over all existing hospital provision. This meant that any disparities in the distribution of that provision were continued in the NHS. For example, for historical reasons London probably had more hospitals in 1948 compared with any other part of the country. The NHS took over these hospitals and, in succeeding years, by increasing the provision of services to all hospitals in a similar way, continued to maintain this disparity.

In the mid 1970s the Government resolved to examine this geographical inequality, as it seemed that patients in some parts of the country had greater access to health services than those in others. The Resource Allocation Working Party reported that there were indeed major differences in access to health care throughout the country. To remedy this they proposed that resources should be distributed to each geographical region of the NHS on the basis of its population size and its mortality experience (the latter as a proxy-measure of morbidity). Over the last decade or so considerable redistribution has occurred, some of it painfully, but the result is a health care system which is now better distributed than it ever has been.

The situation in the UK can be contrasted with those health care systems which do not place a major emphasis on distributive justice. For example, because in the United States fairness, in terms of equality of access, is not a central part of the health care system, there are considerable differences in the allocation of resources between different regions. Thus, there are some parts of the country where it is almost impossible to find a doctor, and other parts in which there are too many.

Social class inequalities

The poorer health of working class people has already been described (Chapter 7). Relative to these health problems, it might be expected that working class people would consult with health services more frequently than middle class. However, there is evidence to suggest that in fact they consult less, relative to their need.

This particular situation was given salience by Tudor Hart's (1971) claim to have discovered an 'Inverse Care Law' in which those with the greatest health need have the poorest services. In essence he was examining the relationship:

$$\text{need} \longrightarrow (\text{availability}) \longrightarrow \text{use}$$

and suggesting that whereas the availability of services should in some reflect need:

$$\text{need} \propto (\text{availability}) \longrightarrow \text{use}$$

they in fact reflected the polar opposite:

$$\text{need} \propto \frac{1}{\text{availability}} \longrightarrow \frac{1}{\text{use}}$$

Need was inversely related to availability and hence to use. In short those with greatest health need had the poorest services and those with least need had the best.

The argument as originally advanced used social class differences as its basis though it has since enjoyed wide currency and is often applied to other seemingly disadvantaged groups such as the old and the chronically ill. The original argument can be broken down into three claims:

1. Working class people have a greater health need than middle class.
2. Working class people have fewer health resources available to them, i.e. need $\propto$ 1/availability.
3. Working class people consequently under-use the health services relative to their need, i.e. need $\propto$ 1/use.

Evidence for the first statement arises from measuring various dimensions of need. While there might be debate about the causes of illness in the different social classes, there is no doubt that major differences in mortality and morbidity (using various measures) are consistently found between the social classes.

Finding evidence to support the second statement is more difficult. In his original argument Tudor Hart used the fact that general practitioner surgeries in working class districts tended to be older than those in middle class districts – which though it might be suggestive is not clear evidence of a difference in the quality of care given – and the fact that as most doctors were recruited from middle class families (some 80% from social classes I and II) they would offer a poorer service to working class people for whom they would have little understanding. Again this second charge is not conclusive although it has some circumstantial evidence to support it in that there are reports of general practitioners giving longer consultations to and covering more problems of middle class patients (Cartwright and O'Brien, 1976). Whether general practitioners from working class backgrounds would respond any differently, however, is open to question.

There are more statistics available for evaluation of the third statement. As was pointed out in Chapter 2 it is now well recognized that the working class under-utilize preventive services such as screening, dental care, postnatal

Table 13.1 GP consultations by social class. (After OPCS, 1986)

Social class	Percentage who consulted in previous 14 days	
	Males	*Females*
I	9	12
II	10	13
IIIn	10	14
IIIm	12	15
IV	13	17
V	13	19

examinations, immunization, etc. For primary health care there are also class differences in consultation rates though these seem to favour the working class (Table 13.1).

However, these figures need to be interpreted in the light of the two other determinants of use: health need and illness behaviour. It might be argued that:

(a) the figures take no account of relative need;
(b) many of the working class consultations are for sickness certificates which they tend to require more often than middle class people.

The effect of these two factors is difficult to establish but relating consultation patterns to measures of morbidity would suggest rough equivalence in consulting rates and allowing for 'certificate consultations' would support the existence of the Inverse Care Law in general practice (Blaxter, 1984).

The problem, however, with evidence which supports the existence of under-utilization relative to health need is that it is not necessarily due to non-availability of facilities (i.e. assumption (2) is not necessary for (1) and (3) to be correct). The argument of the Inverse Care Law is that under-utilization, given a certain level of need, is a reflection of the availability of health care resources whereas, as was argued earlier, it could just as much be a product of different patterns of illness behaviour in working class groups affecting the actual demand for those services, i.e.

$$\text{need} \xrightarrow[\text{behaviour}]{\text{illness}} (\text{demand}) \rightarrow (\text{availability}) \longrightarrow \text{use}.$$

Even if, say, preventive services are offered and made available to a working class population they may not use them. The counter-argument is that the offer and availability of these under-used services is in such a middle class form that there is no congruence with working class values. Thus availability in the form of opening the clinic doors and saying 'come and use it when you need to' reflects more middle class values towards health than working class. It may be necessary to try other means to influence working class behaviour.

Specialty inequalities

Notwithstanding the difficulties in deciding the applicability of the Inverse Care Law to social class and health, the evidence for other areas is more clear. The above has concentrated on social class partly because it was the basis of the original law and partly because it illustrates many of the problems of evaluating and analysing health care statistics. Yet as far as the so-called 'Cinderella' areas of medicine are concerned, particularly mental and physical handicap, geriatrics and parts of psychiatry, the relative lack of very basic amenities such as reasonable food and living conditions constitutes evidence of a distortion of priorities in the provision of care and problems in providing access to good quality care in certain areas of the health service.

● **Is the health care system iatrogenic?**

A patient goes to the doctor with a severe tension headache; the doctor prescribes a month's course of morphine. The therapy is effective because the patient gets better; the patient is now addicted to morphine. This patient benefited from the therapy in one way, but the cost was overwhelming in another. The cost of the health care to this patient is an iatrogenic, that is doctor-induced, disease.

Illich (1974, 1978) has argued that the iatrogenic effects of modern health care are considerably greater than people had realized. He divides his argument into two parts.

Clinical iatrogenesis

First, he argues that clinical iatrogenesis (i.e. doctor-induced disease) is increasing. Thus, in using medical services for a relatively minor health problem, the patient runs the risk of being subjected to investigations and treatments which produce a worse health problem than the original one.

This argument is not new and clinicians have been aware of it for many years. Knowledge is accumulating of the dangers of many drug combinations and of the side effects of treatments and investigations so that it seems reasonable to hope that such forms of iatrogenic disease are kept to a minimum.

Some increase in iatrogenic disease may, paradoxically, represent therapeutic advances which enable some patients to either live longer or more satisfying lives despite having a serious disease. In the end, however, they suffer from the drug therapy rather than the disease which has been kept at bay, and they become a case of iatrogenic disease. Thus, steroid therapy in young people may hold off debilitating illnesses, though in later life the Cushing syndrome which is induced will itself cause problems of medical management.

Social, cultural and structural iatrogenesis

The second and much more striking of Illich's arguments concerns the wider iatrogenic effects of medicine. These have developed to such an extent that: 'The medical establishment has become a major threat to health'.

Illich argues that the general availability of health care to the population has resulted in increasing dependence on doctors. Whereas in the past people had to cope with their own problems and minor symptoms, today they can go to the doctor to talk, to get advice, to obtain drugs, etc.

He therefore argues that providing more health services to meet apparent need is both counterproductive and harmful. Increasing health services creates more need (by reducing people's tolerance thresholds), greater use and in consequence demand for even more services, which in turn is met by increasing resources and so on. In effect a vicious circle of need generating demand, requiring yet more resources which engenders more need, is created.

Some support for this model can be found in the apparent exponential growth in health services in the Western world over the last few decades while self-assessment of health or sickness absence rates seem to deteriorate. It has also been argued that simply making services available encourages increased use. Thus, for example, the different rates of surgical operations found in the USA and the UK seem to bear a closer relationship to the relative numbers of surgeons in these two countries than to any more direct indicators of need for surgery. It has also been found that when general practitioners attempt to reduce the pressure on their surgeries by taking on another partner or extending the length of their clinics the consultation rate in the practice tends to rise and consultations tend to take longer. In short, increased resources allocated to health care often only seem to uncover further demand.

This analysis is the opposite of the Inverse Care Law discussed above. The claim in the latter is that non-availability of health services is detrimental to the health of sections of the population, whereas for Illich it is the converse: that too great an availability of health services is damaging to people's health. Liberal health service provision actually encourages people to use the health service more than they 'really' need. Over time they gradually become dependent on this over-use, feeling it is a necessary part of being healthy. But, claims Illich, this dependence is itself a form of sickness which undermines the good health of autonomous human beings.

The net effect of modern medicine is that people feel themselves to be less healthy than before. The techniques by which medicine achieves this goal are two-fold.

First, it persuades governments and patients that health is something to do with consuming health services. For a government to improve the health of the nation it must invest even more money and persuade people to consume; for individuals to be healthier, they must become greater consumers. Medicine seems to have been very successful in this strategy, in that most Western governments have devoted an increasing proportion of GNP to health care. Even so, costs and demands on the system are still rising inexorably. In Illich's terms, they are rising because the extra amounts spent on the health care system are themselves generating further demand.

In many Western countries about 10% of GNP is now devoted to health care. This means that in those countries, people in the work-force spend about six weeks in every year of their working lives creating the resources which they will then consume to make them healthy. But is this the best way to spend one's life to become healthy? And with further increases in health care costs, will the proportion of people's lives spent creating resources which then can be consumed to make them feel healthy, keep on rising?

The second strategy that medicine has used to achieve its goals is to persuade the population that they can attain standards of health which, in reality, are quite beyond them. For example, the World Health Organization definition of health is that it is 'a state of complete physical, mental and social well-being'. By this definition very few people can be healthy most of the time, but many people might be persuaded that they could be healthier than they are. And is not an important dimension of health the size of the gap between how healthy people think they are and how healthy they think they should be?

The goal of improving one's health status, medicine pleads, can be achieved by consuming all sorts of health services, including drugs. Among the commonest groups of drugs prescribed are minor analgesics and mood altering drugs. It is only recently that some of the side effects and long-term addictive properties of these drugs are being established. Yet for many years, and still today, patients have been persuaded to take tranquillizers, sedatives, hypnotics and stimulants in a vain attempt to make them feel healthier. In Illich's terms the only outcome has been further iatrogenic disease and dependence on doctors.

Not only has medicine seemed content to persuade ill people to consume health services, but also in the attempts to extend illness prevention and health promotion in the last few decades, medicine has tried to persuade everyone that even if they feel healthy, they are still 'at risk'. Thus the healthy population can be persuaded to consume health education and health promotion messages together with screening for various illnesses. In America, annual check-ups are

Illich benefits of animal health check
massively outweighed by ~ve
117 References consequences -

extremely popular despite the lack of evidence as to their overall value. Does any of this improve health? Illich would argue that even if there were some benefits, these are massively outweighed by the negative consequences of medicalizing people's lives. Illness and pain are part of the human condition, and empty promises of relief, and inducements to consume, only exacerbate the situation.

A heroin addict may feel good after taking some of the drug. However, they are not believed to be healthy. In the same way patients who consume health services may obtain temporary relief, but to Illich they have long-term problems. And in the same way that the hard drug problem is tackled, not by punishing the victims but by stopping the drug pushers, the only solution, for Illich, to prevent these damaging effects of health care is the destruction of the medical establishment which is promoting these effects.

Illich's arguments have a simple appeal. They take existing evidence on health service use, and whereas before, increases in health service provision and consumption were praised as signs of improving health standards, Illich turns the tables and points to their negative side. Ideologically Illich would seem to want the population to return to some idyllic state of total self-sufficiency. This is clearly impracticable in modern society, even if it were desirable. Nevertheless, Illich's arguments have resonances in political movements over the last decade or so, which stress individual responsibility and autonomy and the deleterious effects on these aspects of the individual by various forms of welfare provision. Moreover, it is a useful tool by which to analyse health service provision: for example, rather than asking whether a particular screening programme identifies pathology or saves lives, it helps focus on the possible negative effects of medical intervention. Does screening have iatrogenic effects, even on those people shown to be 'healthy'? Does attendance at a screening programme in some way undermine the autonomy and independence of individual patients? If Illich's critique has taught anything, it is that health services can be damaging as well as helpful, and that in future these negative effects should be closely looked for.

• References

Aaron, H. J. and Schwartz, W. B. (1984) *The Painful Prescription: Rationing Hospital Care,* Brookings Institution, Washington

Blaxter, M. (1984) Equity and consultation rates in general practice. *British Medical Journal,* **288**, 1963–1967

Cartwright, A. and O'Brien, M. (1976) Social class variations in health care. In: *The Sociology of the NHS, Sociological Review Monograph,* **22**

Cochrane, A. (1972) *Effectiveness and Efficiency,* Nuffield, London

Illich, I. (1974) *Medical Nemesis,* Calder Boyars, London

Illich, I. (1978) *Limits to Medicine,* Calder Boyars, London

McKeown, T. (1979) *The Role of Medicine,* Blackwell, Oxford

Tudor Hart, J. (1971) The inverse care law. *Lancet,* **i**, 405–412

14

The social basis of disease

In the earlier chapters some contributions which sociology can make to medical practice have been described; knowledge of the importance of social factors in health and disease can be a valuable addition to knowledge of the more traditional biological factors. There is, however, another strand to sociological analysis which challenges the apparently clear distinction between social and biological factors. Put simply, the basis of this second sociological approach is that because all knowledge of the natural world (physics, chemistry, biology, etc.) emerges from within a certain social context, then to a greater or lesser extent that knowledge will be marked by the particular form of the society in which it arose. A good example is the argument that Darwin's theory of evolution, which involved various stratified species and constant competition, could not have arisen outside of a class-ridden, capitalist Victorian society.

The following chapters, in examining the nature of disease and the role of the doctor as social phenomena, will apply this sociological approach (often dubbed the social construction of reality) to medicine (Berger and Luckmann, 1967).

● Defining disease

In any discussion of what constitutes good health the concept of disease has an important part to play. Yet whereas definitions of health involve judgements on the part of both doctor and patient which overtly involve social criteria, e.g. a sense of well-being, a knowledge of the nature and characteristics of disease is peculiar to the medical profession and is usually couched in biological terms. Patients claim to be ill, doctors decide whether they have a disease or not. Yet although doctors rarely have any problem in describing the characteristics of specific diseases, there does seem some difficulty in defining what 'disease' actually is.

One approach is to break the term 'disease' down into its constituent parts, dis-ease. Dis-ease, however, places the definition of disease firmly with the patient and becomes synonymous with the lay concept of illness. This is unsatisfactory as it ignores three factors.

1. The claim of the medical profession to an exclusive skill in identifying disease quite independently of whether the patient feels ill or not.

2. The 'objective' status usually afforded disease as against the more subjective experience of the patient.
3. The existence of pre-symptomatic diseases which do not immediately cause dis-ease.

Another approach which incorporates these factors is to view disease as a 'real' biological phenomenon; this is the traditional medical view. The problem with this approach is three-fold: though the characteristics of specific diseases have been identified, as has been pointed out there is no such agreement on what disease, as a group noun, actually is. Second, great numbers of 'conditions' for which there is no known biological basis, e.g. most psychiatric diseases, are not encompassed within the definition. Third, the non-disease state, by these criteria, is also a biological phenomenon; how is pathology to be separated from physiology?

Although most diseases undoubtedly do have a biological basis this is not sufficient to explain the nature of disease *per se*. An alternative approach to the problem is to start from the idea of what is normal as the definition of normality plays such a crucial role in identifying health and disease.

• Normality in medicine

Put simply, medicine divides bodily functions and processes into physiological and pathological: vision is physiological, blindness is pathological; the growth of epidermal cells is physiological, the growth of cancer cells is pathological: one is normal while the other is abnormal. But how is it that medicine knows whether a cell on a microscopic slide is normal or abnormal? How does medicine know – with such authority – what is normal? The word normal has two meanings.

Statistical

In this sense normal is the 'usual'. It may be given by the average or it may be described by some measure of central tendency.

Does medicine simply rely on numerical occurrences for its definition of normal? It might at first seem so, but there are three difficulties.

1. Statistics can provide no hard and fast boundary between normal and abnormal. They can tell which measurement is more or less normal but not the point at which it becomes 'abnormal'. This problem may not arise in conditions in which the difference between normal and abnormal is clearly distinct, e.g. a disease based on genetic dominance, but most physiological and biochemical parameters are continuously distributed and the exact cut-off point where normal variation becomes pathology is difficult to establish, e.g. diabetes, hypertension, etc.
2. There are so-called pathological phenomena or processes which are statistically normal in some populations. In Western countries, for example, it is actually abnormal to have atheroma-free arteries though such a condition is viewed as healthier than the presence of atheroma.
3. There are many 'abnormal' or 'unusual' biological states and processes in which it would seem absurd to suggest that the patient is diseased. An unusual eye colour, tallness, high IQ, long hair, etc. might all be (biologically) abnormal but still construed as 'normal variations' rather than diseases.

Thus statistical techniques cannot of themselves determine which biological parameters are to be considered as potential bases of disease.

Social or ideal

This is the second way of defining normality. In this sense the normal is that which prevalent social values hold to be acceptable or desirable. This social definition of normality has various advantages over the purely statistical.

The socially acceptable or desirable is very often equivalent to the statistically common. Thus the concept embraces many of those diseases which apparently exist because of their unusualness. Moreover, because the socially acceptable may vary for different communities this definition will accommodate variation in the ascription of disease across social groups. Thus the slowing in psychomotor performance with old age, though a decline from the pattern of youth, is still normal in view of social expectations.

If normality is defined by reference to the socially acceptable then disease becomes a phenomenon which leads to (or may lead to) undesirable social consequences. (The notion of 'responsibility' tends to separate it off from other states which lead to similar consequences.) For many years congenital hyperbilirubinaemia (Gilbert's disease) was viewed as a disease – and was treated – until it was noticed that it had no deleterious effects: it was then retitled a normal variation. In this way, reference to social disadvantage fixes the boundary between normality and abnormality among continuously distributed variables. A blood pressure or a blood sugar level is pathological when it may lead to potentially undesirable consequences for the patient. Difficulty in drawing that boundary reflects the unknown implications of an apparently small rise in blood pressure or blood sugar.

Psychiatric disease, which could not be accounted for by exclusively biological notions of disease, is no longer a problem if a social definition is used. The patient who claims to have two identities contravenes our basic assumptions that people only have one: this break with (our) rationality means the patient is diseased. Or the patient who campaigns against the government in a state in which political dissent and criticism is irrational (in that it contravenes the dominant culture) is similarly held to be mentally ill. The question is not whether such people are 'really' diseased or not, but whether the social criteria by which the disease is established are justified.

It clarifies the debate about whether or not certain 'abnormalities' are to be classified as diseases. Is sickle-cell trait a disease? Only in so far as it confers no advantage on patients or their progeny in a non-malarial country. Is homosexuality a disease? It depends on whether the condition is viewed socially as an abnormality or as a normal variation: conflict over its disease status merely reflects the lack of consensus in society over its social acceptability. Can dyslexia ('word blindness') exist as a disease in a pre-literate society? No, because it confers no social disadvantage.

Use of social criteria to define disease also explains the frequently experienced difficulty of distinguishing between involution and pathology in old age. It is well established that various physiological or involutionary changes occur with age, in particular degeneration of various tissues. Degeneration of tissues, however, is also a characteristic of pathology. In short, disease and involution manifest themselves in similar changes: so how are they to be distinguished?

While biologically these two phenomena are inseparable, they can be socially defined by reference to expectations of old age. Roughly, if the change is expected then it is involution, if it is unexpected it is pathology. Of course our expectations can vary over time and place but, in general, our current perceptions of what old age *should* be like – perhaps mobility and a full life or perhaps slowing and withdrawal – will define the limits of the pathology of the aged as against what is to be construed as 'natural' bodily changes. Sedgewick (1973) pointed out that a fungus growing on wheat is a disease of the wheat only because we want to eat the wheat; if we wished to eat the fungus then it would not be a disease.

In summary, although it is obvious that social values inform political beliefs or legal statutes it is perhaps less apparent that even medicine codifies, in its very subject matter, these same social imperatives. The 'physiological' and the 'pathological' of medicine are only meaningful in a social context which separates the normal from the abnormal. If, every time a doctor diagnoses a disease (pathology) a social norm is manipulated, then medicine, as the next chapter sets out, has a very important social role. The fact that, unlike in the law or politics, the codification of social values in medicine remains for the most part concealed has further implications for the authority and purpose of medicine.

● The biological basis of disease

The reader who approached this chapter with a firm view of the essentially biological character of disease and the doctor's role may feel somewhat confused: surely, it might be argued, diseases are biological and medicine can be practised without playing with politics? The answer is that this claim is correct but incomplete. Thus, whether a particular biological change in the body is socially construed as a disease or not does not detract from the biological character of the change. During menstruation various biological changes occur in the body which are held to be normal; pneumonia is similarly marked by distinctive biological changes, but in the final analysis it is only a disease because of its social label.

In effect, a disease such as pneumonia can be identified (though not ultimately defined) by the presence of certain biological phenomena such as raised temperature, distinctive chest sounds, shortness of breath, leucocytosis, etc. Diagnosis becomes a process of 'pattern recognition' of the biological correlates of disease; moreover the biological character of the disease enables treatment to be appropriately directed. A doctor, therefore, need not be aware of the social basis of disease to practise medicine though this does not mean that medicine is other than a social enterprise.

An analogous situation might be that of architects who look at buildings through their social eye (What is it used for? What are its aesthetics? etc.) but require knowledge of the physical properties of the materials used to construct it. Whether a building is a house, a palace or a cathedral is a social judgement and ultimately cannot be made from the number and quality of stones used to build it. Bricks and mortar only make a building when they are put together with a social purpose. The important point is not that buildings and, by analogy, diseases are exclusively either social or physical/biological phenomena, rather they can be described in either way. Sometimes the biological basis of the disease may be of paramount importance especially when biological/ pharmacological treatments are available, but equally it can be useful to view disease as a social phenomenon for the light it can throw on the role of medicine in society. In this sense politics (with a small 'p') lies at the very heart of medicine.

● References

Berger, P. and Luckmann, T. (1967) *The Social Construction of Reality,* Penguin, Harmondsworth

Sedgewick, P. (1973) Mental illness *is* illness. *Salmagundi,* **20**, 196–224

15

The social role of medicine

If social values underpin disease categories (see Chapter 14), then the encounter between doctor and patient takes on a wider social significance.

• Illness as a deviance

There are usually two parties to the consultation, namely the patient and the doctor. The patient's role in the consultation is to present symptoms to the doctor. As has been pointed out in Chapter 2, feeling unwell is a subjective experience in which various physiological changes have to be interpreted; some changes will be seen as part of normal variation, others will be suggestive of illness. Most of these latter symptoms will be managed at home by the patients themselves or with appropriate social support. Nevertheless there are some symptoms which, because they are inexplicable, unusual or 'deviant' in some way, are brought to the doctor. Thus:

The patient presents personal deviance (1)

The doctor's role on the other hand is to assess the problem with which the patient presents and to give advice and treatment. Traditionally this assessment is effected by taking a history, making an examination and arriving at a diagnosis. But the diagnosis of disease (or the absence of disease) is also, as has been argued in the previous chapter, a means of identifying phenomena which are judged socially abnormal or undesirable. In effect, the doctor is evaluating the patient's problem against criteria of social deviance. Thus:

The doctor evaluates problems by
criteria of socially defined deviance (2)

Putting statements (1) and (2) together a reciprocity in the doctor–patient relationship can be seen. In diagnosis the doctor is juxtaposing what is considered socially deviant against what the patient imagines might be socially deviant. The patient's underlying question when presenting with a symptom, whether it seems organic or psychological, is: 'Am I normal doctor?' or 'Is this abnormal doctor?' to which the doctor replies in terms of criteria based on a wider social norm.

Some examples may help illustrate the argument.

A patient breaks a leg

There will be an accord between doctor and patient with many problems that are presented because they are both aware of the implications of the presenting problem. A broken leg will therefore be recognized, as much by the doctor as by the patient, as a condition requiring treatment.

A patient feels tired and wants to be excused work

The doctor examines the patient, finds nothing wrong and declines to give a sick note. Here the doctor represents the widely held social view that people should work. Not working is a state only to be countenanced if the patient's symptoms might signify some disease which poses a greater threat to social values.

A patient complains of acne

The doctor gives a prescription. In this case the doctor concurs with the patient's belief that this normal skin lesion is socially undesirable and therefore gives appropriate treatment.

A patient complains of insomnia for two nights

The doctor declines to give sleeping tablets. Here the doctor evaluates what is socially acceptable in sleeplessness and concludes that two nights are not long enough to constitute a serious problem. Perhaps if the patient reported two weeks of insomnia it would be treated differently. Undoubtedly these limits would be drawn differently by different doctors but this medical ambivalence only reproduces the general uncertainty about how much sleep loss people should be expected to tolerate.

A patient presents with shortness of breath

The doctor diagnoses chronic bronchitis. Shortness of breath is not of itself significant: it is a normal experience after a period of fast running. What the patient is reporting is that, on this occasion, it seems to occur at inappropriate times. The doctor's task is to judge whether the patient's perception is correct and that the shortness of breath really does interfere to an inappropriate degree with everyday life. If the doctor thinks it does, then the symptoms can be related to 'impaired' lung function and a particular 'pathological process'. On the other hand, similar shortness of breath and the same impairment of lung function in a 90-year-old may not be judged pathological simply because it is not held to be inappropriate for such a patient.

A patient requests that a doctor withholds treatment for a terminal illness

These situations present dilemmas for the doctor because there is conflict of social values. On the one hand the general view in our society is that death is an undesirable outcome. (Again, it is worth noting that death is a social event as well as a biological one. In certain situations in various communities – the old in a nomadic tribe, the martyr, the political prisoner who starves himself – death may be seen as a desirable end because it serves to reinforce the integrity or social goals of community.) In Western society, strenuous attempts will be made to maintain life, though even these may vary from country to country. In the USA, for example, doctors may stress the maintenance of life, at whatever cost, more than their colleagues in the UK.

On the other hand, freedom from pain and suffering and the right of patients as individuals to have some say in their future are, like the undesirability of death, widely held social values. Thus when the patient wants to die it falls on the doctor to resolve the conflict between the importance of human life and of personal autonomy. In some situations drugs can relieve the pain and the patient's right to a part in the decision can be reduced if it is believed that because of the imminence of death he or she is not 'rational' (because the desire to die offends fundamental social values it is easy to label it as 'irrational'). The dilemma arises for the doctor when there is a certainty that the patient 'really' does want to die.

● The doctor as agent of social control

Because the doctor is constantly juxtaposing social values against personal ones, it can be seen that medicine is performing a social function as well as its more obvious therapeutic one. Specifically, the evaluation of personal deviance in terms of social values means that medicine is intimately involved in maintaining social consensus and coherence. In this role of arbiter of social values, medicine therefore acts as an institution of social control and the doctor as an agent of social control. By constantly reaffirming the boundaries of social normality the doctor serves as a support for the maintenance of social order.

The professions

This social control function is not unique to medicine: it has been, and still is, carried out by other occupational groups.

The Church

Especially in earlier times the Church was the ultimate judge in matters of social values and behaviour. The Church legislated on acceptable social conduct and at the interpersonal level accepted the penitent's confession of offences against these rules. The confession was an admission of personal deviance which received affirmation and absolution from the priest who drew from his wider knowledge of what was and what was not admissible thought and behaviour.

The Law

With the decline of religion in modern times the explicit rules governing social conduct have increasingly been taken over by the Law. People are believed to have full responsibility for their actions and when they transgress the law they must be judged and punished. As with the Church, the Law both constitutes a body of knowledge (the rules) and a procedure by which those who have broken those rules have their innocence or guilt judged and acted upon. Though the defendant's plea in a court of law forms a part of the assessment of the case, the ultimate judgement of innocence or guilt is independent of the defendant's belief about the rightness of his own actions. The judgement is, in effect, a juxtaposition of the defendant's personal behaviour (established by the court) and socially accepted rules of conduct embodied in the Law.

Medicine

It is fairly obvious that the Law is an institution of social control, but perhaps less clear for medicine, partly because deviance in medicine is usually couched in terms of abnormal biology rather than behaviour, which tends to conceal its social basis. Even so, as has been argued earlier, underlying these biological phenomena are fundamental social values.

Thus like law, medicine is a body of knowledge embodying social values (disease) and incorporates a procedure by which patients are judged ill or well by the doctor. As in law, this judgement occurs independently of the patient's own beliefs. These beliefs may be of value in reaching a diagnosis, but it is often the case that patients are judged ill even though they believe themselves to be well, e.g. in presymptomatic screening tests, or are judged well even though they see themselves as ill. Thus, in the same way that the Church and the Law uphold norms of social conduct, medicine too, as one of the three 'great' professions, can be seen to be upholding social values and, to a certain extent, social conduct (though the latter is gaining more emphasis).

To argue that medicine is engaged in 'social control' is not to say that doctors are some sort of secret policemen. All it means is that medicine, like many other apparently innocuous social activities such as bringing up children, reading a textbook, going to school, watching television, etc. controls aspects of knowledge and ideas which support the existing social order.

The sick role

Once it is established that medicine is an institution of social control, many other aspects of the sociology of medicine tend to fall into place. The 'sick role', for example, which was described in Chapter 2 as a benefit which can be conferred on the patient by the doctor, can now be seen in context (Parsons, 1951). The four expectations and obligations really only make sense if viewed in their relationship to medicine's social role.

The patient is temporarily excused normal social roles
The power to legitimate sickness absence is vested in the medical profession and provides an essential element in social control in that commitment to work is a central value of our society.

The patient is not held responsible for his illness
The ascription of responsibility is an important factor in differentiating a medical from a legal problem. Law holds miscreants responsible for their actions whereas medicine does not. For example, whether murderers are to be viewed as criminals to be punished by prison or patients to be treated in a psychiatric hospital depends on whether or not they were responsible for their actions. Similarly if a shoplifter can establish that due to some hormonal imbalance, e.g. during the menopause, she was not responsible for her theft, she becomes a medical rather than a legal problem.

In many ways it is somewhat arbitrary whether people are held responsible for their actions or not. Ultimately it is underpinned by a philosophical debate over free-will and determinism rather than a dispute which can be settled with recourse to 'evidence'. Because of this the boundary between medicine and law is often blurred and it is open to medicine to invade areas of human conduct traditionally maintained by legal mechanisms. Indeed it has been claimed that medicine is increasingly intruding into new areas of human conduct and using its powerful social position to legislate on appropriate and inappropriate behaviour. In part this has been the result of medicine taking over the role of other agencies such as the Church and the Law; it is also the result of medicine extending its definition of health problems to include more and more psychological and social aspects (see Chapter 9). This process of 'medicalization', as it is called, has been discussed in Chapter 13 and it is further explored below.

A further aspect of non-responsibility concerns preventive medicine. Seemingly one of the benefits that medicine can confer on the patient is freedom from feeling responsible for the illness. Unlike many other agencies of the welfare state there is apparently no need for the patient to feel guilt or failure at having to consult a doctor. This undoubtedly helps explain why many 'problems of living' are brought to the doctor rather than to other professionals (such as social workers, marriage guidance counsellors, housing officers, etc.), because the latter may be seen to hold the patients, at least in part, responsible for their actions or current situation.

However, as mentioned above the denial of responsibility is always somewhat arbitrary and it is quite possible to 'blame' patients for having disease. Cigarette smokers who present with lung cancer or ischaemic heart disease could be held to be partly responsible for their predicament if they knew beforehand of the dangers of smoking, yet still continued.

On the other hand, if patients are held responsible for their health this may encourage them to take preventive measures. It is increasingly suggested that the days in which governments could improve the nation's health without the active involvement of the people, e.g. in sanitation, in providing clean water, etc. are now passed. Prevention, it is argued, now rests with individuals who must change unhealthy behaviour patterns if they are to avoid ill health. (The emphasis on personal responsibility for health is also, of course, a political issue as it makes important assumptions about the control people can exert over their own lives in contemporary society.) There is thus a stress on personal responsibility in the language of disease prevention. A by-product of the success of this approach, however, might be to place a decreasing inclination to consult the doctor for these 'preventable' diseases because of the blame and guilt attached to them.

This problem can be seen in those medical problems which already have a measure of responsibility attached to them. These range from attempted suicides who, inasmuch as they are directly responsible for their condition, often seem to receive less sympathy from medical staff (though if they are 'really' ill with, say, severe depression then attitudes might change) to the guilt surrounding venereal diseases for which, through extramarital sexual intercourse, the patient is held responsible. In the latter the feelings of guilt are catered for by anonymity during treatment while strenuous attempts are made publicly to 'de-stigmatize' the disease so help will be sought early.

The patient must want to get well

The patient must cooperate with the doctor
Both of these obligations serve to uphold the legitimacy of the social control functions of medicine while at the same time ensuring that they are effective. Just as defendants must recognize the authority of the court (otherwise they are in contempt) so the patient must defer to the authority of the doctor. Failure to

do so involves removal of the benefits of the sick role such that the patient is not considered ill so much as a 'malingerer'.

● **Explaining the place of medicine**

The fact that medicine seems to have an important role in the maintenance of social order has not been an end point of social analysis, but an important starting point. Because of the extent and pervasiveness of medicine in modern society, it seems to have a special place in the explanation of the latter. Sociologists, however, have not been agreed – but who would expect them to be? – on what that place should be, and different views are widely debated. While this debate is not of direct relevance to the actual practice of medicine, which presumably is the purpose of many readers of this book, this final section will briefly summarize some of the broad sociological positions on the role of medicine in society. Overall these various positions can be seen as offering different answers to the question: 'What is the effect of the social control function of medicine?'

Functionalism

During the early post-war years sociologists supported a model of society which argued that its different components existed in harmony and mutual support. Society was characterized by a broad consensus about social values and, within this schema, medicine had a particular role in managing and controlling deviance in the form of illness, which might otherwise threaten or undermine the central value consensus. From this perspective, the effect of social control was that deviance was contained and consensus maintained.

Parson's notion of the sick role, which has been covered in the preceding section, was an essential component of this system. The sick role is, above all, a mechanism for maintaining social order by ensuring that the deviant illness state is properly managed and processed.

The right wing critique

The social control functions of medicine have been extending in modern society such that medicine now pervades a far greater part of everyday life than it ever did. This position, the medicalization of everyday life, has been criticized by some social scientists who see inherent dangers in this process.

At its mildest, this critique would argue that there is a great danger in becoming too reliant on experts. Zola (1972), in arguing that medicine was an institution of social control, makes this point. The danger of relying on experts is that individual citizens become deskilled and their ability to act autonomously is compromised.

Illich (1974) takes this argument further when he claims that the medicalization of society has become a positive danger to the health of all citizens (see Chapter 13). Medicine, in taking over responsibility for people's health, undermines their independence and reduces their ability to cope. The result is a society of medical addicts. The political New Right (Green, 1985) have similarly argued (mostly with less passion than Illich) that the medical care, particularly in the context of its provision through the welfare state, has reduced individual autonomy, independence, and ability to cope.

For functionalism, the social control function of medicine ensured the suppression of deviance which might otherwise threaten social stability. For the right wing critics, the social control function of medicine has extended beyond suppressing deviance to suppressing individuality itself. In this sense medicine has become a repressive force used by central authorities for maintaining a bland social consensus, which denies individual rights and autonomy.

The left wing critique

The left wing critique of functionalism, mainly drawn from a Marxist perspective, also argues that medicine has been used to suppress people, but not in the same sense as the right wing critique. For the political left, the whole organization of modern society is flawed. Late capitalism, and its concomitant social relations of production which pervade the work place are, it is argued, also maintained by medicine. Thus, despite its protestations to the contrary, medicine is used in modern society to maintain inequality between social groups, and ensure that the uneven distribution of power is not threatened (Doyal, 1979).

This criticism ranges from the attack on medicine as an agency of State suppression (Navarro, 1976) to the charge that even the doctor–patient relationship involves the consolidation and maintenance of capitalist values, which themselves ensure the continuation of social groups with and without power in its widest sense (Waitzkin, 1979).

The left wing critique, like the right wing critique, sees medicine as a repressive force but, unlike the latter, believes it is not individuals in general who are being suppressed but particular social groups.

Constructivism

Over the last decade a new analysis of social control has appeared. Whereas the traditional critiques of functionalism have argued that social control by medicine has essentially been a negative force used to repress individuals or social groups, this new perspective argues that social control may be a positive force used, not to suppress, but to create.

The argument starts with the emergence of biomedicine at the end of the eighteenth century when disease became located to specific anatomical structures and hence illness could yield to a reductionist analysis (Foucault, 1963). Biomedicine treated the patient's body as a machine, as an object. This effect of medicine is criticized by both the political right and left as somehow objectifying 'real' people. But alternatively, the objectification of the individual at this time can be seen as the first step in the actual creation of individuality and the 'construction' of the modern notion of the body as a discrete and analysable object (Foucault, 1977). The constructivist position is that reality does not exist independently of perception, and that therefore the new biomedicine created its own objects and its own reality.

In similar fashion, from the beginning of the twentieth century medicine began increasingly to focus on psychological and social diseases. In this analysis the body became seen as inhabiting a social as well as physical space; in consequence it became a social as well as physical phenomenon (Armstrong, 1983).

Since the 1950s these elements of an extended patient identity have been reinforced and developed. Biomedicine, through its techniques of clinical examination, continues to fabricate a discrete and analysable body, but in recent years the mind and social context of that body have been integrated to construct a psychosocial identity for patients (Armstrong, 1984). In the last few decades medicine has investigated a series of new phenomena and problems which have as their common goal and assumption the existence of a patient as a subjective 'whole person': the actual practice of medicine has therefore created and reinforced the independence and existence of a unique patient identity. Thus, whereas for the other critics of functionalism described above the invasion of medicine into more 'private' areas of people's lives has been seen as an undesirable and pernicious influence, the constructivist would argue that it is only by examining and analysing these components of patienthood that identity itself is constructed.

Debates about the social role and effects of medicine will no doubt continue. However, these various analyses have, like the recent challenges to the long-term benefits of the eighteenth century idea of Enlightenment, brought out the idea that in some ways the biomedical approach to illness may have been a 'mistake'. This charge is as yet a vague suggestion, particularly as there is no obvious alternative for the explanation and management of illness in society. Nevertheless the future of medicine in its various forms can only be analysed in the context of a society of which it is part, and with which it has reciprocal relations.

● **References**

Armstrong, D. (1983) *Political Anatomy of the Body: Medical Knowledge in Britain in the 20th Century,* Cambridge University Press, Cambridge

Armstrong, D. (1984) The patient's view. *Social Science and Medicine,* **18**, 737–744

Doyal, L. (1979) *The Political Economy of Health,* Pluto Press, London

Foucault, M. (1963) *The Birth of the Clinic: An Archeology of Medical Perception,* Tavistock, London

Foucault, M. (1977) *Discipline and Punish: The Birth of the Prison,* Penguin, Harmondsworth

Green, D. G. (1985) *Working Class Patients and the Medical Establishment,* Gower, Aldershot

Illich, I. (1974) *Medical Nemesis,* Calder Boyars, London

Navarro, V. (1976) *Medicine Under Capitalism,* Prodist, New York

Parsons, T. (1951) *The Social System,* Free Press, New York

Waitzkin, H. (1979) Medicine, superstructure and micropolitics. *Social Science and Medicine,* **13**, 601–609

Zola, I. K. (1972) Medicine as an institution of social control. *Sociological Review,* **20**, 487–504

Bibliography

Aaron, H. J. and Schwartz, W. B. (1984) *The Painful Prescription: Rationing Hospital Care,* Brookings Institution, Washington

Abel-Smith, B. (1976) *Value for Money in Health Services,* Heinemann, London

Anderson, J. A. D. (ed.) (1979) *Self-Medication,* MTP Press, Lancaster

Anderson, M. (1980) *Approaches to the History of the Western Family: 1500–1914,* Macmillan, London

Arber, S. (1987) Social class, non-employment, and chronic illness: continuing the inequalities in health debate. *British Medical Journal,* **294**, 1069–1073

Arber, S., Gilbert, G. N. and Dale, A. (1985) Paid employment and women's health: a benefit or a source of role strain? *Sociology of Health and Illness,* **7**, 375–400

Armstrong, D. (1979) The emancipation of biographical medicine. *Social Science and Medicine,* **13**, 1–8

Armstrong, D. (1983) *Political Anatomy of the Body: Medical Knowledge in Britain in the 20th Century,* Cambridge University Press, Cambridge

Armstrong, D. (1984) The patient's view. *Social Science and Medicine,* **18**, 737–744

Balint, M. (1964) *The Doctor, His Patient and the Illness,* Pitman, London

Banks, M. H. and Jackson, P. R. (1982) Unemployment and risk of minor psychiatric disorder in young people: cross-sectional and longitudinal evidence. *Psychological Medicine,* **12**, 789–798

Banks, M. H., Beresford, S. A. A., Morrell, D. C. *et al.* (1975) Factors influencing demand for primary medical care in women aged 20–44. *International Journal of Epidemiology,* **4**, 189–195

Becker, H. S. (1963) *Outsiders: Studies in the Sociology of Deviance,* Free Press, London

Beecher, H. R. (1959) *Measurement of Subjective Responses,* Oxford University Press, Oxford

Bentham, G. (1988) Migration and morbidity: implications for geographical studies of disease. *Social Science and Medicine,* **26**, 49–54

Berger, P. and Luckmann, T. (1967) *The Social Construction of Reality,* Penguin, Harmondsworth

Berkman, L. F. and Syme, S. L. (1979) Social networks, host resistance, and mortality: a nine year follow-up study of Alameda County residents. *American Journal of Epidemiology,* **109**, 186–204

Blaxter, M. (1976) *The Meaning of Disability,* Heinemann, London

Blaxter, M. (1984) Equity and consultation rates in general practice. *British Medical Journal,* **288**, 1963–1967

Bloor, M., Samphier, M. and Prior, L. (1987) Artefact explanations of inequalities in health: an assessment of the evidence. *Sociology of Health and Illness,* **9**, 231–264

Blumhagen, D. (1980) Hyper-tension: a folk illness with a medical name. *Culture Medicine and Psychiatry,* **4**, 197–227

Brown, G. W. and Harris, T. (1978) *Social Origins of Depression: A Study of Psychiatric Disorder in Women,* Tavistock, London

Brown, G. W., Davidson, S., Harris, T. *et al.* (1977) Psychiatric disorder in London and North Uist. *Social Science and Medicine,* **11**, 367–377

Bury, M. (1982) Chronic illness as biographical disruption. *Sociology of Health and Illness,* **4**, 167–182

Cartwright, A. and Anderson, R. (1981) *General Practice Revisited,* Tavistock, London

Cartwright, A. and O'Brien, M. (1976) Social class variations in health care. In *The Sociology of the NHS, Sociological Review Monograph,* **22**

Cartwright, A., Hockey, L. and Anderson, J. L. (1973) *Life Before Death,* Routledge and Kegan Paul, London

Cassel, J. (1976) The contribution of the social environment to host resistance. *American Journal of Epidemiology,* **104**, 107–123

Channer, K. S., O'Connor, S., Britton, S. *et al.* (1988) Psychological factors influence the success of coronary artery surgery. *Journal of the Royal Society of Medicine,* **81**, 629–632

Clark, A. and Fallowfield, L. J. (1986) Quality of life measurements in patients with malignant disease: a review. *Journal of the Royal Society of Medicine,* **79**, 165–169

Cochrane, A. (1972) *Effectiveness and Efficiency,* Nuffield, London

Conrad, P. (1985) The meaning of medicalisation: another look at compliance. *Social Science and Medicine,* **20**, 29–37

Craig, T. K. and Brown, G. W. (1984) Goal frustrating aspects of life event stress in the aetiology of gastrointestinal disorder. *Journal of Psychosomatic Research,* **28**, 411–421

Crawford, R. (1977) You are dangerous to your health: the ideology and politics of victim-blaming. *International Journal of Health Services,* **7**, 663–679

Creed, F. H. (1981) Life events and appendicectomy. *Lancet,* **i**, 1381–1385

Creed, F. H. (1985) Life events and physical illness: a review. *Journal of Psychosomatic Research,* **29**, 113–124

Culyer, A. J. (ed.) (1983) *Health Indicators,* Martin Robertson, Oxford

DHSS (1976) *Sharing Resources for Health in England: Report of the Resource Allocation Working Party,* HMSO, London

DHSS (1987) *Promoting Better Health: The Government's Programme for Improving Primary Health Care,* HMSO, London

Dohrenwend, B. S. and Dohrenwend, B. P. (eds) (1981) *Stressful Life Events and their Context,* Produst, New York

Donovan, J. (1984) Ethnicity and health: a research review. *Social Science and Medicine,* **19**, 663–670

Doyal, L. (1979) *The Political Economy of Health,* Pluto Press, London

Dubos, R. (1980) *Man Adapting,* Yale University Press, New Haven

Dunnell, K. and Cartwright, A. (1972) *Medicine Takers, Prescribers and Hoarders,* Routledge and Kegan Paul, London

Durkheim, E. (1933) *The Division of Labour in Society,* Macmillan, New York

Durkheim, E. (1952) *Suicide: a Study in Sociology,* Routledge and Kegan Paul, London

Egbert, J. A., Battit, G. E., Welch, C. E. *et al.* (1964) Reduction of postoperative pain by encouragement and instruction of patients. *New England Journal of Medicine,* **170**, 825–827

Foucault, M. (1963) *The Birth of the Clinic: An Archeology of Medical Perception,* Tavistock, London

Foucault, M. (1977) *Discipline and Punish: The Birth of the Prison,* Penguin, Harmondsworth

Freidson, E, (1970) *Profession of Medicine,* Dodd Mead, New York

Fry, J. (1983) *Present State and Future Needs in General Practice,* MTP Press, Lancaster

Goffman, E. (1961) *Asylums: Essays on the Social Situation of Mental Patients and Other Inmates,* Penguin, London

Goffman, E. (1963) *Stigma: Notes on the Management of Spoiled Identity*, Penguin, London

Goode, W. J. (1960) Encroachment, charlatanism and the emerging profession: psychiatry, sociology and medicine. *American Sociological Review*, **25**, 902–914

Gove, W. R. (1973) Sex, marital status and mortality. *American Journal of Sociology*, **79**, 45–67

Gove, W. R. (1976) Societal reaction theory and disability. In *The Sociology of Physical Disability and Rehabilitation* (ed. G. L. Albrecht), University of Pittsburgh Press, Pittsburgh

Graham, H. (1987) Women's smoking and family health. *Social Science and Health*, **25**, 47–56

Green, D. G. (1985) *Working Class Patients and the Medical Establishment*, Gower, Aldershot

Hannay, D. R. (1980) Religion and health. *Social Science and Medicine*, **14a**, 683–685

Harris, A. I. (1971) *Handicapped and Impaired in Great Britain*, HMSO, London

Helman, C. (1978) 'Feed a cold starve a fever' – folk models of infection in an English suburban community and their relation to medical treatment. *Culture Medicine and Psychiatry*, **2**, 107–137

Henderson, S. A. (1980) A development in social psychiatry: the systematic study of social bonds. *Journal of Nervous and Mental Diseases*, **168**, 63–69

Henry, J. P. and Cassel, J. C. (1969) Psychosocial factors in essential hypertension. *American Journal of Epidemiology*, **90**, 171–200

Higgins, P. C. (1980) *Outsiders in a Hearing World: A Sociology of Deafness*, Sage, London

Hollandsworth, J. G. (1988) Evaluating the impact of medical treatment on the quality of life: a 5-year update. *Social Science and Medicine*, **26**, 425–434

Holmes, T. H. and Rahe, R. H. (1967) The social readjustment rating scale. *Journal of Psychosocial Research*, **11**, 213–218

Honigsbaum, F. (1979) *The Division in British Medicine*, Kogan Page, London

Hunt, S., McEwen, J. and McKenna, S. P. (1986) *Measuring Health Status*, Croom Helm, London

Illich, I. (1974) *Medical Nemesis*, Calder Boyars, London

Illich, I. (1978) *Limits to Medicine*, Calder Boyars, London

Ingleby, D. (ed.) (1981) *Critical Psychiatry: The Politics of Mental Health*, Penguin, London

Jenkins, R. (1985) Sex differences in minor psychiatric morbidity: a survey of a homogeneous population. *Social Science and Medicine*, **20**, 887–899

Jewson, N. K. (1976) Disappearance of the sick-man from medical cosmologies, 1770–1870. *Sociology*, **10**, 225–244

Johnson, T. J. (1972) *Professions and Power*, Macmillan, London

Jones, I. G. and Cameron, D. (1984) Social class analysis: an embarrassment to epidemiology. *Community Medicine*, **6**, 37–46

Jones, K. and Fowles, A. J. (1984) *Ideas on Institutions: Analysing the Literature on Long-Term Care and Custody*, Routledge and Kegan Paul, London

Kasl, F. V. and Ostfield, A. N. (1984) Psychosocial predictors of mortality among the elderly poor: the role of religion, well-being and social contact. *American Journal of Epidemiology*, **119**, 410–423

Katz, S., Ford, A. B., Moskowitz, R. W. *et al.* The Index of ADL: a standardized measure of biological and psychosocial function. *Journal of the American Medical Association*, **185**, 914–919

Kleinman, A., Eisenberg, L. and Good, B. (1978) Culture, illness and cure. *Annals of Internal Medicine*, **88**, 251–259

Komaroff, A. L. (1984) Acute dysuria in women. *New England Journal of Medicine*, **310**, 368–375

Koos, E. (1954) *The Health of Regionsville: What the People Felt and Did About It,* Columbia University Press, New York

Kronenfeld, J. J. (1979) Self-care as panacea for the ills of the health care system: an assessment. *Social Science and Medicine,* **13A,** 263–267

Last, J. M. (1963) The clinical iceberg: completing the clinical picture in general practice. *Lancet,* **ii,** 28–30

Lemert, E. (1967) *Human Deviance, Social Problems and Social Control,* Prentice Hall, Hemel Hempstead

Lewis, J. and Meredith, B. (1988) Daughters caring for mothers: the experience of caring and its implications for professional helpers. *Ageing and Society,* **8,** 1–21

Linn, M. W., Linn, B. S. and Stein, S. R. (1982) Beliefs about causes of cancer in cancer patients. *Social Science and Medicine,* **16,** 835–839

Littlewood, R. and Lipsedge, M. (1981) *Aliens and Alienists: Ethnic Minorities and Psychiatry,* Penguin, London

Locker, D. (1981) *Symptoms and Illness: The Cognitive Organization of Disorder,* Tavistock, London

Locker, D. (1983) *Disadvantage and Disability,* Tavistock, London

Marmot, M. G. and Syme, S. L. (1976) Acculturation and coronary heart disease in Japanese Americans. *American Journal of Epidemiology,* **104,** 225–247

Marmot, M. G. *et al.* (1975) Epidemiological studies of coronary heart disease and stroke in Japanese men living in Japan, Hawaii and California. *American Journal of Epidemiology,* **102,** 514–525

Marmot, M. G., Adelstein, A. M. and Bulusu, L. (1984) Immigrant mortality in England and Wales, 1970–78. *OPCS Studies on Medical and Population Subjects,* No. 47, HMSO, London

McDowell, I. and Newell, C. (1987) *Measuring Health Status: A Guide to Rating Scales and Questionnaires,* Oxford University Press, Oxford

McKeown, T. (1979) *The Role of Medicine,* Blackwell, Oxford

Mechanic, D. (1962) The concept of illness behaviour. *Journal of Chronic Diseases,* **15,** 189–194

Mechanic, D. and Volkart, E. H. (1960) Illness behaviour and medical diagnosis. *Journal of Health and Human Behaviour,* **1,** 86–94

Melzack, R. and Wall, P. D. (1965) Pain mechanisms: a new theory. *Science,* **150,** 971

Meyer, R. J. and Haggerty, R. J. (1962) Streptococcal infection in families: factors altering individual susceptibility. *Pediatrics,* **29,** 539–549

Moser, K. A., Fox, A. J. and Jones, D. R. (1984) Unemployment and mortality in the OPCS longitudinal study. *Lancet,* **ii,** 1324–1328

Moser, K. A., Goldblatt, P. O., Fox, A. J. *et al.* (1987) Unemployment and mortality: a comparison of the 1971 and 1981 longitudinal study census samples. *British Medical Journal,* **294,** 86–90

Nathanson, C. A. (1977) Sex, illness, and medical care: a review of data, theory and method. *Social Science and Medicine,* **11,** 13–25

Navarro, V. (1976) *Medicine Under Capitalism,* Prodist, New York

Parsons, T. (1976) *The Social System,* Free Press, New York

Patrick, D. L., Morgan, M. and Charlton, R. H. (1986) Psychosocial support and change in the health status of physically disabled people. *Social Science and Medicine,* **22,** 1347–1354

Pennebaker, J. W. (1984) Accuracy of symptom perception. In *Handbook of Psychology and Health,* vol. IV, (eds A. Baum *et al.*), Erlbaum, New Jersey

Pill, R. and Stott, N. C. H. (1982) Concepts of illness causation and responsibility: some preliminary data from a sample of working class mothers. *Social Science and Medicine,* **16,** 315–322

Platt, S. and Kreitman, N. (1984) Unemployment and parasuicide in Edinburgh, 1968–82. *British Medical Journal,* **289,** 1029–1032

Rawles, J. M. and Haites, N. E. (1988) Patient and general practitioner delays in acute myocardial infarcts. *British Medical Journal*, **296**, 882–884

Robinson, D. and Henry, S. (1977) *Self-Help and Health*, Martin Robertson, London

Rose, G. and Marmot, M. (1981) Social class and CHD. *British Heart Journal*, **45**, 13–19

Rosenhan, D. (1973) On being sane in insane places. *Science*, **179**, 250–258

Rosenthal, M. (1987) *Dealing with Medical Malpractice: The British and Swedish Experience*, Tavistock, London

Safilios-Rothschild, C. (1970) *The Sociology and Social Psychology of Disability and Rehabilitation*, Random House, New York

Safilios-Rothschild, C. (1976) Disabled persons' self-definitions and their implications for rehabilitation. In *The Sociology of Physical Disability and Rehabilitation* (ed. G. L. Albrecht), University of Pittsburgh Press, Pittsburgh

Scambler, G. (1984) Perceiving and coping with stigmatizing illness. In *The Experience of Illness* (eds R. Fitzpatrick et al.), Tavistock, London

Scambler, G. and Hopkins, A. (1986) Being epileptic: coming to terms with stigma. *Sociology of Health and Illness*, **8**, 26–43

Schoenbach, V. J., Kaplan, B. H., Fredman, L. *et al.* (1986) Social ties and mortality in Evans County, Georgia. *American Journal of Epidemiology*, **123**, 577–591

Schur, E. (1971) *Labelling Deviant Behaviour*, Harper and Row, London

Scott, R. A. (1969) *The Making of Blind Men*, Russell Sage, London

Scull, A. T. (1971) *Decarceration*, Prentice Hall, Englewood Cliffs

Sedgewick, P. (1973) Mental illness *is* illness. *Salmagundi*, **20**, 196–224

Szasz, T. S. (1962) *The Myth of Mental Illness*, Paladin, St Albans

Szasz, T. S. and Hollender, M. H. (1956) A contribution to the philosophy of medicine: the basic models of the doctor–patient relationship. *Archives of Internal Medicine*, **97**, 585–592

Townsend, P. and Davidson, N. (1982) *The Black Report*, Penguin, London

Townsend, P., Davidson, N. and Whitehead, M. (1988) *Inequalities in Health*, Penguin, London

Tuckett, D., Boulton, M., Olson, C. *et al.* (1985) *Meetings Between Experts: An Approach to Sharing Ideas in Medical Consultations*, Tavistock, London

Tudor Hart, J. (1971) The inverse care law. *Lancet*, **i**, 405–412

Turner, R. M. (1978) Recurrent abdominal pain in childhood. *Journal of the Royal College of General Practitioners*, **28**, 729–734

Waitzkin, H. (1979) Medicine, superstructure and micropolitics. *Social Science and Medicine*, **13**, 601–609

Waldron, I. (1976) Why do women live longer than men? *Social Science and Medicine*, **10**, 240–262

Weiner, C. (1975) The burden of rheumatoid arthritis: tolerating the uncertainty. *Social Science and Medicine*, **9**, 97–104

Wells, N. (1987) *Women's Health Today*, OHE, London

WHO (1980) *International Classification of Impairments, Disabilities and Handicaps*, World Health Organization, Geneva

Williams, A. (1985) Economics of coronary artery bypass grafting. *British Medical Journal*, **291**, 326–329

Wood, P. (1975) *Classification of Impairments and Handicap*, World Health Organization, Geneva

Zola, I. K. (1972) Medicine as an institution of social control. *Sociological Review*, **20**, 487–504

Zola, I. K. (1973) Pathways to the doctor: from person to patient. *Social Science and Medicine*, **7**, 677–689

Index